TROPICAL HOUSES

Living in Nature in Jamaica, Sri Lanka, Java, Bali, and the Coasts of Mexico and Belize

TIM STREET-PORTER

CLARKSON POTTER/PUBLISHERS
NEW YORK

PUBLISHED BY CLARKSON POTTER/PUBLISHERS, NEW YORK, NEW YORK. MEMBER OF THE CROWN PUBLISHING GROUP.

RANDOM HOUSE, INC. NEW YORK, TORONTO, LONDON, SYDNEY, AUCKLAND WWW.RANDOMHOUSE.COM

CLARKSON N. POTTER IS A TRADEMARK AND POTTER AND COLOPHON ARE REGISTERED TRADEMARKS OF RANDOM HOUSE, INC.

PRINTED IN HONG KONG

DESIGN BY RICHARD FERRETTI

LIBRARY OF CONGRESS CATALOGING-IN-PUBLICATION DATA
STREET-PORTER, TIM.
   TROPICAL HOUSES : LIVING IN NATURE IN JAMAICA, SRI LANKA, JAVA, BALI, AND THE COASTS OF MEXICO AND BELIZE / TIM STREET-PORTER.
   INCLUDES BIBLIOGRAPHICAL REFERENCES AND INDEX.
   1. ARCHITECTURE, DOMESTIC.   2. ARCHITECTURE, TROPICAL.   I. TITLE.
NA7117.T74 S77   2000
728'.37'0913—DC21   00-020333
ISBN 0-517-70462-5

10 9 8 7 6 5 4 3 2 1

FIRST EDITION

PAGE 1 A late Majapahit door, flanked by a ceiling wax palm and East Indonesian figures, welcomes visitors to the entry courtyard of Villa Bayugita at Begawan Giri resort in Bali. PAGE 2 The decoratively painted wall of a traditional residence in west Sumatra. PAGE 3 A corner of the garden of the elegant Tandjung Sari hotel in Sanur. PAGE 4 An opening in the staircase wall of a villa in Careyes, Mexico, framing a terracotta pot and a view of the harbor. PAGES 6–7 The Ayung River's horseshoe curve at Sayan in Bali, one of the island's most celebrated views. Since this photograph was taken, the Four Seasons Sayan Hotel was built on a portion of this site. OPPOSITE Glazed tiles project slivers of sunshine onto palm-shaded walls in the courtyard of the Villa Oriente in Careyes (architect: Jean-Claude Galibert). OVERLEAF Rain falls on newly planted rice seedlings in the mountains of Bali.

CONTENTS

INTRODUCTION

ONE OF THE PLEASURES OF LIVING in the tropics is an awakening of the senses that brings us closer to nature. Here between the equatorial latitudes of Cancer and Capricorn lies a broad band of the earth's ocean and land surface where the sun hovers directly overhead, generating an environment of perpetual warmth and fertility. In volcanic tropical regions, the soil is especially rich in nutrients, and a twig plunged into the ground will sprout leaves within days.

Distinctions between indoors and out evaporate in the tropics, and walls become redundant—except for privacy. Without this confinement the house is free to expand into the landscape, to be open to passing breezes, allowing the sights, sounds, and scents of nature to waft through its living spaces. As one becomes sensitized to these air currents, one develops new awareness: of when rain is imminent, of the earthy fragrances released with its arrival, of the sudden warm breath when the sun reappears. For rain is a daily feature of life in the tropics. Here, unlike elsewhere in the world, getting wet is a pleasant experience. Raindrops are warm; the sun usually reappears soon after the shower; and wet clothes are dry again within minutes.

Living with nature in the tropics opens a world of sensual experiences. In Bali, for instance, bathing is a sybarite's delight. We take our morning shower in a space enclosed by a stone wall for privacy and extending out beyond the thatched roof beneath which we had slept. Here, in a miniature enclosed garden, with the sun filtering through a frangipani tree, we tranquilly observe butterflies dancing in and out of view, a lizard on the wall, as we dry ourselves and sip morning tea.

Bedtime in the tropics is another magical experience, again nowhere more so than in Bali. Sleeping as one does in a grass-roofed pavilion with no walls, the sounds and scents of the night mingle freely with our dreams. In this enchanted environment, cocooned in a net-canopied four-poster, we are hyperaware of the tropical landscape outside, and there are times when the full moon gives it an ethereal visibility. The nocturnal air is densely punctuated by an orchestra of frogs and cicadas.

THE VERNACULAR AND DESIGNING IN THE TROPICS

THE TASK OF THE DESIGNER OF HOUSES in the tropics is to establish a sense of harmony with nature. The challenges are many. Living close to nature brings with it an appreciation of natural materials, and most of the houses in this book, with the exception of those designed in European-influenced colonial styles, are built with thatched roofs and of wood, bamboo, or adobe. Natural ventilation

PRECEDING PAGES An early-morning view of Gunung Agung from the terrace of Hugo Jerreisati's retreat in Iseh in Bali. OPPOSITE Outdoor shower at the Begawan resort in Bali. The limestone was imported from the neighboring island of Sumba.

is essential because of high temperatures and humidity. This is accomplished by designing high ceilings with vents that allow heat to escape and air to circulate constantly. (Even chair backs are made of woven cane with holes that allow air through to cool the occupant.) Architects such as Marco Aldaco of Mexico have been known to camp out on the site to learn the best places to catch prevailing winds before committing pencil to paper. These breezes are utilized in the design to create airflows through the house. Designed in this way, a house is an organism and becomes an extension of nature.

While conventional air-conditioning should be superfluous in a well-designed, naturally ventilated tropical house, there is still the problem of humidity, which can be destructive to books and fabrics, especially during the wet season. Houses built in this manner do need at least one air-conditioned room (it might be the bedroom, or the office, or just a storeroom). This is where books, business papers, and clothes can be preserved against mildew.

In some parts of the tropics, and particularly in Southeast Asia, houses are traditionally raised on stilts to catch the air currents, as well as to provide extra security against unwanted wildlife, and often to protect against monsoon flooding.

Deep eaves help to keep the sun away from the edges of the building, where heat can accumulate in the paving and radiate from there into the interior. Verandahs, protected by eaves wide enough to require the support of a row of colonnade, keep the interior cool and provide additional living space in the fresh air. Glass is replaced with wood-louvered windows, which filter strong light and reduce glare during the brightest hours but allow breezes to waft through.

Wood (or bamboo) construction has another advantage besides its sympathetic appearance: Tropical regions are often susceptible to earthquakes. Both wood and bamboo have natural flexibility, and buildings built with these materials are usually the ones that survive.

Thatched roofs proliferate throughout the tropics. Interestingly, particular constructional techniques in some countries match those in other lands far away, suggesting that ideas were communicated via early migrations and trading routes. The Mexican Pacific Coast *palapa,* for instance, is thought by some to have originated in the Philippines, whereas the thatched roofs a few hundred miles away in Mexico's Veracruz were first built by escaped slaves who brought the idea from Africa. Thatched roofs are irresistible to today's designers in Southeast Asia and Mexico: Wonderful to live with, they suit the vernacular and are inexpensive in terms of both labor and materials.

Because of its availability and low cost wood was traditionally used for housing in the tropics. Houses were not necessarily regarded as permanent. Parts could be easily replaced—thatched roofs and bamboo structures have a lifespan of only a few years—and, if necessary, the entire house could be moved from one loca-

OPPOSITE The finely detailed roof of a residential pavilion in Batujimbar. Traditional Balinese architecture is distinguished by a clarity and honesty of constructional detailing and a fine articulation of elements. Natural, organic materials are used throughout. Alang-alang grass is stitched to bamboo ribs to form shingles and lashed to bamboo rafters. Post and beams of polished coconut, a wood noted for its attractive grain, are fitted together either by tongue and groove or mortise and tenon jointing.

tion to another. More permanent stone construction was reserved for religious structures.

In indigenous housing, courtyards are created as areas defined by individual pavilions, some open—the better to enjoy the surrounding spaces and fragrant landscaping. The traditional Balinese residential compound is a good example: a series of pavilions linked by courtyards, and surrounded by a high garden wall. Today's version, epitomized by Made Wijaya's home and studio in Bali (see page 133), continues this tradition.

Most of the houses featured on these pages, although equipped with all the usual amenities such as plumbing, electricity, and electronics, nonetheless share many design features with the indigenous housing from which they have evolved: the romance of the past allied with modern convenience. While aesthetics and nostalgia play a part in contemporary vernacular design, architects are sensible enough to synthesize functional traditions that have successfully evolved over time, developing an architecture that responds to the climate and local topography and makes best use of local materials.

COLONIAL STYLE

THE LURE OF HIGHLY PROFITABLE TRADE in spices, gold, and other desirable items drew the Europeans—first the Portuguese in the sixteenth century, then the Dutch and English in the seventeenth—around the Cape of Good Hope to the Indian Ocean and Southeast Asia, and across the Atlantic to the Caribbean. Developing and controlling these lucrative markets led to extensive colonization in both these regions.

As coastal trading settlements became established, suitable housing became necessary for the administrators and traders who lived and worked in them—a home far away from home. Later, the often grand houses of plantation owners became a feature of the rural landscape farther inland. The inspiration for these houses—whether in Goa, Batavia (now Jakarta), Antigua, Penang, Rangoon, Madras, or Manila—came from remembered architectural styles back in Lisbon, London, or Amsterdam. There was little reference to local traditions. To achieve comfort in a climate quite unlike anything experienced in northern Europe, however—with intense heat, humidity, and periodically fierce monsoon rains—a little tweaking was necessary. Such design flourishes as louvered windows, ceiling fans, and verandahs protected by broad eaves transformed a typical Dutch or English villa into a hybrid architecture of reasonable practicality and idiosyncratic charm.

OPPOSITE A well-preserved house in the historic Bali Aga (pre-Hindu) village of Bayung Gede, showing an array of traditional materials: bamboo roofing tiles, wood, and mud walls. OVERLEAF A balcony at the Casa dos Estrellas (left), overlooking Costa Careyes harbor; the rustic balustrade is crafted from local wood. A corner of the eighteenth-century Kerta Gosa pavilion (right), surrounded by a moat, in Klungkung in East Bali—the island's ancient hall of justice. Its ceilings are covered with concentrically arranged illustrations relating an elaborate traditional fable.

JAMAICA

JAMAICA IS NO MERE SLEEPY VACATION ISLAND. It is a real country, in some ways like Bali. It's the same size, approximately 150 miles long and 50 miles in width, and, like Bali, has a strong sense of identity—vividly expressed in its unique culture and religion. The latter, Rastafarianism, developed since Jamaica's independence in 1962 as a proud affirmation of the country's African roots.

Jamaica is also one of the world's most beautiful islands, with exquisite beaches, mountains, jungle, and an abundance of streams, rivers, and waterfalls. The island was discovered by Christopher Columbus in 1494, who claimed it for Spain. There was no gold in Jamaica, but the Spanish established plantations to supply the ships that crisscrossed between Europe and the Americas. Jamaica was plundered by British pirates and eventually captured by the British navy in 1655. Nicknamed the "Pearl of the Caribbean," Jamaica remained a British colony for three hundred years.

The island's architectural legacy is mostly British. They established sugarcane plantations run from a Great House, which resembled in function the great haciendas of Latin America. Always placed on the highest ground on the estate, these houses would visually dominate and take advantage of cooling breezes. They were

PRECEDING PAGES Linda Garland designed this sybaritic open-air bathroom (left) at the Goldeneye resort, surrounded by exotic landscaping and a high fence for privacy. Enjoying the Caribbean spray (right) from the verandah of a Trident Hotel villa near Port Antonio. RIGHT A wooden gingerbread house (top) in Black River, built in the early 1900s, when wooden fretwork was popular as a decorative motif. The 1960s villas at the Trident Hotel (middle), designed in a traditional style with wood-shingle roofs and attractive fretwork flourishes. One of the stylish, privately owned villas (bottom) at Round Hill resort, near Montego Bay. OPPOSITE Adele Astaire's breezy bedroom in her villa at Round Hill.

mostly built during the Georgian period, which is reflected in their facades and interior details. The features that distinguish them from French Caribbean buildings include a front porch, a strict symmetry of facade, and occasional Palladian flourishes. Louvered windows were often incorporated into the facades as a nod to the tropics, and verandahs appeared on side and rear elevations.

Smaller houses, usually built of wood, better reflect a tropical lifestyle. Wood louvers replace glass, and the verandah features more prominently, becoming the main living space. As elsewhere in the Caribbean, life is lived more outdoors than in. Also, a house can be more than one building—the kitchen and bathroom are often separate structures.

In the 1920s yachts began cruising into picturesque Port Antonio, a seaside town in the prettiest corner of the island, nestled in lush tropical hills and surrounded by spectacular beaches. In these yachts were among the world's wealthiest and most glamorous: J. P. Morgan, William Randolph Hearst, and Clara Bow.

In the 1950s and 1960s Jamaica enjoyed a tourist renaissance, and a new resort near Montego Bay became a popular watering hole for the international glitterati. Of the many stylish resorts along the island's north coast, Round Hill, developed by Jamaican John Pringle, was the most exclusive. Its compound of twenty-seven privately owned villas and a thirty-six-room hotel made it the perfect "hideaway" for socialites and celebrities. One of the first to buy a cottage was Noël Coward, who then persuaded friends to follow his example. Regular visitors, many with their own villas, included Bill and Babe Paley, Adele Astaire, John and Jackie Kennedy, Grace Kelly, Alfred Hitchcock, Clark Gable, Gloria Vanderbilt, and Princess Margaret. Round Hill today is as popular as ever.

An hour's drive to the east, Noël Coward built Firefly, his hilltop residence with sweeping views up the coast. Ian Fleming lived minutes away at Goldeneye, now an Island Outposts resort run by Jamaican entrepreneur Chris Blackwell. Patrick Leigh Fermor wrote about a visit to Goldeneye in the 1940s in *The Traveller's Tree:* "Here on a headland, Commander Ian Fleming has built a house called Goldeneye that might serve as a model for new houses in the tropics. Trees surround it on all sides except that of the sea which it almost overhangs. Great windows capture every breeze, to cool, even on the hottest day, the large white rooms. The windows that look toward the sea are glassless, but equipped with outside shutters against the rain: enormous quadrilaterals surrounded by dark wooden frames which enclose a prospect of sea and cloud and sky, and tame the elements, as it were, into an ever-changing fresco of which one can never tire."

LEFT Borrowing their roof color from the water at this Jamaican beauty spot, the artfully designed Blue Lagoon villas edge a coral reef near Port Antonio. They date back to the 1960s, when this area was a high-society enclave.

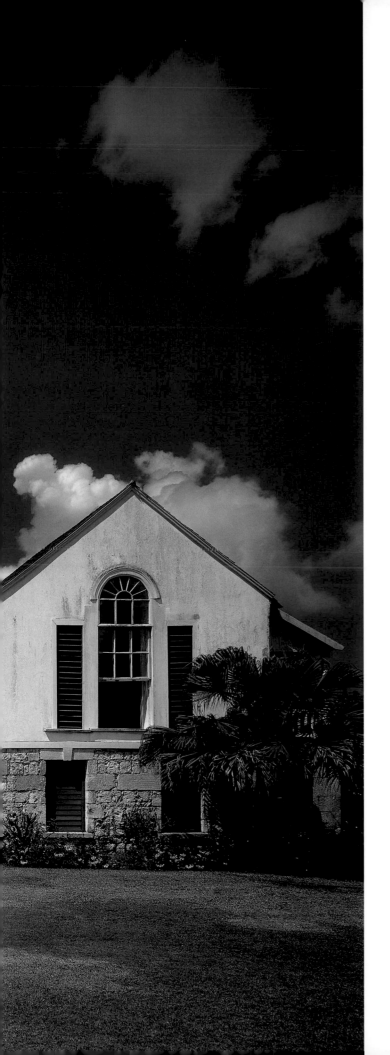

GOOD HOPE

GOOD HOPE, AN EIGHTEENTH-CENTURY Great House (local parlance for a country seat, or hacienda) in the parish of Trelawny, sits serenely on a lofty hilltop overlooking its estates, which spread across the Queen of Spain valley. Fields dotted with cattle are shaded by ancient hardwood trees, and the hazy profile of the Cockpit Mountains dominates the distant horizon. It is a landscape little changed in two hundred years. Not quite visible from the house are the estate's prodigious and commercially successful crops of papaya, *uniq* citrus (a local cross between tangerines and grapefruit), akees (vegetables traditionally mashed with codfish—Jamaica's answer to kedgeree, and its national dish), and anthuriums.

Good Hope was first settled in 1744, and its elegant cut-stone Great House was built soon after by a Lieutenant Colonel Williams. The estate was then bought in 1766 by John Thorpe, who expanded it from 1,200 to 9,000 acres, built five sugar factories, a dam, a canal with waterwheels, and a 300-bed hospital for the 3,500 resident slaves.

Over many years the estate's fortunes changed. Businessman Tony Hart, the current owner, first saw the dilapidated property when it came on the market in 1989. His first thoughts "were that here was a part of the country's history, that it was dete-

LEFT The imposing eighteenth-century Palladian facade of Good Hope's Great House, which overlooks its extensive estates, is a classic example of Jamaica's colonial heritage. A nod to tropical design can be seen in the louvers flanking the central sashes in each window grouping.

riorating, and that it should be saved." Hart already owned 800 acres adjoining Good Hope, and he was able to combine these with its 1,200 remaining acres, and then arrange a consortium with four investor friends, including entrepreneur Chris Blackwell, to finance the restoration of the house and estate. Hart's wife, Sheila, worked with local decorator Ky-Ann Walker to refurbish the interiors. Three years of work and substantial expense were needed to reset this jewel in its grandly rustic setting.

Good Hope operates today as an elegant ten-bedroom rentable villa run by Hart's son Blaise. Visitors are greeted by well-polished original-cedar floors and a variety of plantation furniture, much of which is also original to the house, and the rest chosen to match as closely as possible. Most of this furniture, as well as the wall paneling in the bathrooms, is of native mahogany. Berbice chairs mingle with mahogany tables and sideboards decorated with colorful arrangements of crotons, anthuriums, hibiscus, and sprigs of bougainvillea. The walls are hung with oil paintings and lithographs of Jamaican scenes, as well as views of the Good Hope estate.

Of particular note is a Palladian structure in the garden, just behind the main building, which reveals itself in the middle of the tropical foliage. This is the old countinghouse, built high for protection, and reached by a flight of stone steps. Now a guest suite, its louvered windows allow the breeze to filter through white-lace mosquito netting that drapes a voluptuous canopied bed.

LEFT The garden entrance (top) is flanked by large pots; the countinghouse guest suite is a few steps behind the camera's position. This long-established lily pond (middle), flanked by a massive tree and vines, has survived a number of successive owners. The Palladian facade of the old countinghouse (bottom); set in the back garden, it is now the prize guest suite. OPPOSITE The verandah adjoining the living room offers a view of the Queen of Spain valley, shrouded here in early morning mist.

OPPOSITE The interior of the old countinghouse, converted into a suite, with a bathroom screened behind the bed. ABOVE RIGHT The living room, furnished with a mixture of native mahogany furniture and comfortable couches. The open roof space above collects hot air as it rises, keeping the occupants cool. RIGHT Polished cedar floors and mahogany furniture greet visitors in the entry hall. Wood louvers between interior spaces promote the flow of air through the house.

WOODSTOCK

ALSO OWNED BY TONY HART, WOODSTOCK was bought in 1983 as a hobby farm and retreat. A farmhouse high in the mountains behind Montego Bay, it was built in 1911 as a cattle farm to provide lumber and livestock for sugar factories in the lowlands. (Oxen were used to pull carts to and from the factories in these earlier times, and beef was needed to feed the workers.)

Woodstock, like Good Hope, was dilapidated when Hart bought it and is now much restored. The verandah which runs the length of the house is used as an outdoor living room and is shared with a colony of birds that constantly come and go, attracted by a long line of feeders hanging from the eaves. Among these daily visitors is the long-tailed hummingbird, Jamaica's national bird, its distinctive six-inch twin tails hanging expressively from its tiny body.

The Georgian-style house is kept cool by wood louvers set into the fenestration, by airy interior spaces open to the roof, and its strategic placement on a hilltop to catch prevailing breezes.

LEFT The rustic exterior of Woodstock, looking much like a Georgian country house but surrounded by a deep verandah. The house is perched on a hilltop overlooking its properties and takes advantage of cooling breezes. OVERLEAF One of the charms of unmanicured country estates is an element like this: a gateway (left) to a long-abandoned garden retained as a conceptual landscaping feature. Woodstock's entry portico (right), with the fretted woodwork that has long been a decorative feature on the island. Note the wood louvers flanking the main windows.

ITOPIA

SURROUNDED BY RAIN FOREST, ITOPIA IS the home of author-director Perry Henzell, who directed the classic reggae movie *The Harder They Come,* and his artist wife, Sally. Tucked away in the hills behind Runaway Bay on the north coast, it has been both family home and creative retreat since the Henzells discovered it more than twenty years ago. Perry has written several novels in the house, often not leaving for weeks at a time. It is a writer's paradise with a real sense of distance from the outside world. There is no telephone, and drop-in visitors are rare. Situated in a rural area of mazelike lanes unencumbered by street names or house labeling, it is almost impossible to find.

The Henzells christened the house Itopia as a play on the Rastafarian expression "I and I," which means "one with God." It is built of local cut stone and dates back to the early eighteenth century. It was originally the dower house to Cardiff Hall Great House, the seat of the Blagrove family, who moved here from England just after Oliver Cromwell conquered Spanish Jamaica. The estate was for a while one of the island's biggest suppliers of sugarcane.

LEFT Outbuildings at the back of the house melt into the jungle that surrounds the property. These buildings are used as a studio; the verandah overlooks the back garden.

The house, in true tropical style, maximizes the use of natural ventilation to keep everything cool. English-style sash windows are bordered by louvered openings which encourage airflow, and interior spaces are open to the roof pitch to allow heated air to rise above head level.

The original plan was to repaint the interiors, but Sally, who is partner with her son in Jake's, a hotel on the south coast (which she designed and decorated), fell in love with the mix of colors revealed as layers of old paint were stripped away. The richly decorative effect that she settled on was achieved by the unorthodox technique of scraping at the walls with a machete. She has decorated with an eclectic mix of family furniture, local antiques, and junk-shop finds accumulated over the years.

LEFT The garden view of the vine-covered rear of the house (top); the tiled roof is split into three bays. A view of the garden from the back porch (middle), which is a favorite haven for the family dog. The cut-stone front elevation of Itopia (bottom). OPPOSITE The Henzells' living room is bright and eclectic: Floral fabrics, blooms from the garden, and huge vines glimpsed through the French doors blend with the unusual wall treatment. OVERLEAF A corner of the living room looking through to the study (left), showing the scraped-wall treatment. Interior designer Sally Henzell refashioned the downstairs guest bathroom into a grotto (right), using rocks from the property, recycled curved windows from a display cabinet, and colored glass, which she added to the glazed sections of the windows.

STRAWBERRY HILL

CHRIS BLACKWELL'S MEMORIES OF STRAW-berry Hill, a Blue Mountains estate hovering three thousand feet above Kingston, go back a long way. "I used to come here," the entrepreneur reminisces, "for Sunday tea with my mother when I was a little boy, and I've always had a sentimental feeling about this place." Strawberry Hill originated as an eighteenth-century coffee plantation, and Blackwell bought the property in 1972 to use as a personal retreat. It was here that Blackwell's protégé, reggae artist Bob Marley, recuperated from gunshot wounds after a politically motivated attempt on his life. In 1988 its Great House was destroyed by Hurricane Gilbert. Blackwell then began making plans to develop the estate into a traditionally Jamaican planter-style hotel.

A bit of history: Blackwell is known to many as the founder, promoter, and producer of Island Records, which he ran entirely by instinct, signing only music which he believed in—preferably Jamaican. His most notable achievements with Island were discovering Bob Marley and the Wailers and propelling their music into the international mainstream. Island's varied roster of artists—Bob Marley, U2, Steve Winwood, Melissa Etheridge, Grace Jones, and the Cranberries—grew and succeeded expo-

LEFT Designed by Jamaican architect Ann Hodges, Chris Blackwell's own cottage is separate from the hotel's villas, in a private garden. Hodges used vernacular idioms, including decorative fretwork, to enliven the facade.

nentially, and Blackwell eventually sold the label to Polygram in 1987 for $300 million.

Having divested himself of Island Records, Blackwell then went into the hotel business with his new company, Island Outpost. His first hotels in Miami, beginning with the Marlin, were a key to the revival of South Beach. He then turned his attention back to Jamaica, involving himself in a string of resorts around the island, working to revitalize local economies and culture—he uses only local resources. The first of these was Strawberry Hill.

To develop the estate as a resort, he hired architect Ann Hodges, who had grown up in Jamaica and trained in London. Hodges created a new spin on Jamaican traditional architecture, using vernacular pitched roofs, decorative fretwork, and overlarge roof eaves extended to a point of exaggeration, allowing guests to sit outdoors and remain comfortably dry during rainstorms.

The twelve guest cottages are modeled on traditional Jamaican chattel houses, and the interiors are also typically Jamaican. Furnishings include planter's chairs and mahogany four-poster beds shrouded with white-muslin mosquito netting. The landscaping, anchored by the many mature trees on the property, and with a wealth of rare tropical plants and flowers, is developing into a botanical garden.

In 1963 Noël Coward wrote in his diary, "We drove to the Strawberry Hill Inn, which has the most fabulous views on each side and is really attractive. Quite small, good food and a glorious garden with everything imaginable growing. There was a fragile new moon and the lights of Kingston glittered like rhinestones." It could have been written yesterday.

LEFT In the spring, the back lawns of Strawberry Hill (top) are covered in yellow blossoms. The restaurant is decorated with fretwork openings with a bamboo motif (middle); broad sheltering roof eaves surround the building. A two-story villa nestles in the tropical foliage (bottom). The design is modeled on traditional Jamaican chattel houses. OPPOSITE This verandah of the villa seen on page 44 overlooks the Blue Mountains and a hilltop church.

SRI LANKA RESEMBLES A GIANT MANGO set into the Indian Ocean next to the southeastern coast of India. Rich in history and legend, it is very much an independent country and not to be confused with its vast neighbor. Even its religions—Buddhism predominates—distinguish it from Hindu India. Sri Lanka changed its name (from Ceylon) in the 1970s after achieving independence from British rule; it was referred to as Lanka in the two-thousand-year-old Hindu epic, the *Ramayana.* Concurrently, the Romans knew it as Taprobane, and to Muslim traders (and readers of the voyages of Sinbad in the *Arabian Nights*) it was known as Serendib.

Sri Lanka is rich in archaeological remains, which are concentrated within its so-called Cultural Triangle made up of three former capital cities. The earliest two are Anuradhapura (eleventh century and earlier) and the short-lived, but wonderful, Polonnawura (twelfth century), which rivals the best Buddhist statuary in India. The third is the stately mountain city of Kandy, last of the Sinhalese capitals. This remained an independent kingdom, due to its inaccessibility, during successive Portuguese and Dutch occupations, relinquishing its status to the British when they took over the island early in the late eighteenth century. The latter opened up Kandy to the coast with a new road and transformed it into a fashionable resort—complete with a top-class botanical garden—so that residents of Colombo, now the capital, could recover from the coastal heat. It was later to become a favorite refuge for Viscount Mountbatten.

Close to Kandy but at a higher altitude is Nuwara Eliya, center of the important tea plantation district and a popular hill station for the

PRECEDING PAGES In Colombo, a flamboyant example of the turn-of-the-century Sri Lankan gingerbread style (left). An airy bedroom (right) in Illukitaya, Hans Hoefer's converted plantation house in the hills behind Galle. It opens onto the central courtyard, to the left. Wood-fretted window treatments are traditional. The bed is surrounded by terra-cotta tiles and raised on a plinth. TOP Hans Hoefer's garden, showing the elegant, characteristically Sri Lankan house design: a broad verandah, widespread eaves, with a lantern light overhead to allow hot air to escape the interior, as well as to let light in. ABOVE Another gingerbread fantasia, this time an updated version, attached to a recently built hotel near Galle. OPPOSITE The seventeenth-century Old Town of Galle, seen from a greensward that extends along the oceanfront. (Charles Hulse's house, facing the same greensward, is just out of frame to the left.) A Buddhist temple is in the foreground, and a lane extends back toward the seventeenth-century Dutch Reformed church.

British, who dressed it up into an amusing pseudo-English village. Here we find charmingly archaic clubs filled with hunting trophies and billiard rooms, a hotel where at bedtime a hot-water bottle is still placed between the sheets, and an assortment of half-timbered "stockbroker Tudor"–style houses from the 1920s.

Sri Lanka's architecture has long been affected by its location in the midst of east-west trade routes, which go back in time to ancient Greece and Rome. However, it was the Portuguese—who built forts and churches on the island and introduced pitched and tiled roofs, as well as courtyards, and the Dutch, who built the Old Town of Galle within the Portuguese fort—who contributed most to the local design vocabulary. The best-known contemporary architect is Geoffrey Bawa, who borrowed from the island's primarily Portuguese colonial legacy and promoted concepts of tropical living, banishing glass from windows and encouraging a domestic life which embraced the outdoors.

Sri Lanka's graceful towns, richly varied landscape, and exotic wildlife have attracted a sprinkling of notables who loved it enough to become permanent residents, including, in earlier days, the photographer Julia Margaret Cameron, and, more recently, the novelist (and scuba diver) Arthur C. Clarke.

Sri Lanka's recent history since its separation from British rule has been marked by civil war, and sporadic outbreaks of violence have been sufficient to prevent the growth of mass tourism on the island. This is bad for the economy, but for the adventurous, Sri Lanka is an ever-increasing rarity: a beautiful, culturally rich island only lightly touched by tourism. The historic Old Town in Galle, for instance, is a World Heritage site confined within the walls of the seventeenth-century fort set on a beautiful ocean promontory. Here visitors can enjoy, and have to themselves, the magical aura of a place unchanged for over half a century: a miniature Asian version of Havana.

Along the southwestern coast of Sri Lanka lie a series of resort villages stretched between Colombo, the capital, and Galle, which is also a picturesque fishing town and regional center. East of Galle, the road that runs along the south coast quickly becomes less developed, at least for tourism, making it all the more appealing as a location for tropical retreats.

RIGHT Hans Hoefer's arcaded central courtyard in Illukitaya, a feature introduced to Sri Lanka by the Portuguese, with an ornamental pool and fountain. The courtyard works like inner lungs, promoting airflow through the surrounding bedrooms and living spaces, the doors of which are surmounted by open fretwork. A lantern light can be seen hovering over the roof of the main living space in the middle of the photograph.

CHARLES HULSE
RESIDENCE

THE OLD TOWN OF GALLE, FIVE TINY BLOCKS long and three wide, was built by the Dutch in the eighteenth century within the massive fortifications laid in place by the Portuguese a century earlier. It occupies a promontory with the Galle harbor on one side and the modern town behind. The charming fort is still the hub of local government, and each morning thousands of schoolchildren dressed in colorful uniforms mingle with parasol-toting office workers as they pour in through the fort's imposing main gate.

With views of the nonstop cricket played with unique Sri Lankan fervor on the greensward that lies between it and the seawall, Charles Hulse's house and its setting resemble a tropical version of Cornwall. Facing southwest, it catches the steady ocean breezes. The horizon, visible from upper-floor windows, stretches all the way to Antartica.

The house was built in the early nineteenth century, during the British occupation—its deeds date back to 1840. It was a rooming house when Hulse bought it, its interior spaces divided with plywood partitions: It had been rented to schoolteachers at the college behind the house, police officers, and

LEFT Charles Hulse's upstairs dressing room. Layers of lattice and louvers filter ocean breezes. The window beyond has views out over the seawall to an oceanic horizon.

lawyers at court. Hulse found it while house-shopping for a friend. After a quick inspection, he decided that his own needs came first. When his friend asked him, "Charlie, is there anything in the fort for me?" he truthfully replied, "No, Sylvia, not a thing!"

No longer a plywood rabbit warren, the house is filled with antiques accumulated in Sri Lanka and France by Charles and his late friend, the writer Gordon Merrick. Ground-floor rooms are linked by carefully enlarged openings, allowing layered views through the house. Outside, Hulse paved a tiny patio with white-painted cement, linking this with an outdoor dining space reclaimed from the old kitchen. Here the exterior walls and roof were simply removed, leaving a grid of beams overhead, which at night frames the stars. The patio is shaded with tropical foliage and is used as an outdoor living room—ideal for its owner's two most popular pastimes: reading and cocktails with friends.

Hulse split the upstairs floor into two zones. Guest bedrooms occupy the rear of the house, while at the front a large study and the master bedroom and bathroom enjoy views of the grassy downs, the stone wall of the fort, and the sea. Windows throughout are kept open so that ocean breezes can flow through the rooms.

OPPOSITE The entry hall in the Hulse residence. The floor is painted white to bring light through into adjacent living rooms. RIGHT A corner of the sitting room (top), looking beyond to the entry lobby. Living spaces all interconnect visually. The furniture, mostly the result of antique shopping, is from the region. The living room (middle) has a generously high ceiling and exemplifies the characteristic, well-designed tropical colonial room. An upstairs guest bedroom, with a traditional Sri Lankan canopied bed (bottom).

ABOVE LEFT In this corner of the drawing room, the window is kept open except in rainstorms. Note the characteristic air vent above the glazing. LEFT The drawing room has a variety of tropical furniture. The rattan open weave is useful for ventilation, and the use of green brings a sense of the foliage outside into the house. OPPOSITE The interiors are layered from space to space. The entry passage is glimpsed here through the opening behind the rattan couch. Behind this is a lattice-screened exterior window, which allows light, air, and sound from the oceanfront park outside to waft through.

TANGALLE

NAMED AFTER A NEARBY FISHING VILLAGE on a remote stretch of the south coast two hours east of Galle, Tangalle was owned by the late artist Douglas Johnson, who died in 1998. His house is preserved with his attractive furnishings and artworks and is available for rent through the Sunhouse in Galle.

Johnson spent six months of the year at Tangalle. Summers were spent in the south of France, a season of gallery openings and portrait sittings for notables such as the Getty family, Lord Weidenfeld, and Prince Albert of Monaco. Then he was back to an annual six month idyll on the Indian Ocean, where the nearest phone was six miles away.

After ten years of renting houses around Sri Lanka, Johnson heard about the remote charms of Tangalle from friends: a simple bungalow in the local Sinhalese style with Portuguese flourishes. The tile-roofed bungalow has a perfect seafront location, a colonnaded verandah, and is surrounded by a large coconut grove. A simple path

LEFT The porch, flanked by built-in stuccoed benches, of a guest cottage in Tangalle painted in bright colors. Wooden posts support a tiled roof. Broad eaves lend extra protection in storms.

through the grass leads to a gate that opens directly onto an empty, beautiful beach lined with coconut palms.

The shady interiors are kept cool with flagstoned floors and the ocean breeze, which drifts through the shuttered, glassless window openings. The verandah is furnished with a variety of antique local furniture that Johnson liked to rearrange almost daily. Great care and time went into the white-gray-white color scheme, which gives the house a sophistication beyond that of the holiday home. Furniture is mostly Dutch from the nineteenth century, made from local jackwood, ebony, and madun, and caned to allow the all-important flow of air. Remote as it is, the house is visited only by house guests, fishermen (selling their daily catch of lobster), and an occasional iguana.

LEFT A gate (top) leads from the house to a perfect isolated beach, empty except for the odd passing fisherman. From the beach a path (middle) leads across a lawn to an attractive traditional Sinhalese bungalow with a colonnaded verandah and expansive terrace. The terrace (bottom). Armchairs and a table are grouped around a built-in Portuguese-style stuccoed couch. OPPOSITE Traditional planter's chairs are placed to enjoy the view of the lawns and sea beyond. Vertically louvered window openings strike a distinctively graphic note.

THE SUNHOUSE

NESTLED IN A HILLSIDE OVERLOOKING THE Galle harbor, on a quiet lane that begins in town at the colonnaded fish market and ends with the Governor's Mansion, the Sunhouse is an eighteenth-century cottage—the former home of a Scottish cinnamon merchant—recently converted into a discreet guest house. It owes much of its appearance and distinctive style to American decorator Dick Dumas, who bought the property in 1991, opened up the rooms to their present configuration, and added a new wing and decorative flourishes to the interior. These were all happily retained by the new owner, Geoffrey Dobbs, an Englishman with a collection of Sri Lankan properties, most of which can be rented. Dobbs bought the Sunhouse in 1996 together with its furniture, adding more, and opening it as a hotel with six guest suites plus a grand upper-floor suite with all-around views over the tree-tops to the coast.

The hotel has a breezy, Caribbean atmosphere, with a colonnaded dining terrace that looks out onto a garden landscaped with a grove of frangipani, which in turn overlooks a pool. An air of civilized informality makes the Sunhouse the least institutional of guest houses, and its visitors feel like house guests.

LEFT An ornate Sri Lankan canopied bed in the upstairs master suite, which runs the length of the upper floor, with sunrise views of the jungle on one side and sunset vistas of the ocean and the old fort on the other.

ABOVE LEFT The garden view of the eighteenth-century Sunhouse, with its full-length verandah and upper floor, which contains the master suite. The garden is shaded by a large tree, which is surrounded by a continuous bench. LEFT The Sunhouse living room. Beyond, a passage leads to the garden. The striped doorway was decorated by previous owner Dick Dumas. OPPOSITE The master suite sitting room, visited by the Sunhouse cat. Beyond are the access stairs and a treetop view along the coast. OVERLEAF The back garden is filled with frangipani trees and a pool.

LEFT A lunch-table setting from the garden with a frangipani centerpiece, strewn jasmine, and palm leaves. TOP The colonnaded dining loggia faces the garden and swimming pool. Food is brought up daily from the historic fish and vegetable markets at the end of the street. ABOVE Sewing is carried out on a venerable Singer machine on the terrace overlooking the front courtyard.

TAPROBANE

OF THE SIZABLE STREAM OF EUROPEAN adventurers, artists, and romantics who have sought out their personal Edens in the tropics, one of the first was the Count de Mauny-Talvande. His first trip to Ceylon, as it was then called, was in 1912 with the tea magnate Sir Thomas Lipton. This visit, his first experience of the tropics, clearly made a deep impression. He returned after the First World War on a mission to find "the one spot which, by its sublime beauty, would fulfill my dreams and hold me there for life."

It was ten years before he found his paradise: a tiny islet on the south coast of Ceylon. Set in a huge bay, this rocky outcrop covered with lush foliage rises from the water just beyond a broad sandy beach. For the count it epitomized every child's fantasy of a South Seas tropical island. On seeing this vision, the intrepid count waded across (even at high tide, the water rises only to the chest) and, in his words, "sat for a long while on a boulder overlooking the sea, wishing that this island lost in the Indian Ocean were mine; picturing and planning what I should do with it. I felt my heart beating with

LEFT Count de Mauny-Talvande's dream. A short flight of steps welcomes visitors to the Isle of Taprobane. The steps are a short, waist-deep wading distance from the shore. The 1930s octagonal house fits neatly onto the island's crest, just allowing space for terraces and patios on all sides.

the overwhelming desire to find in it peace, the nearest thing to happiness. Yes, it must be the home which I had dreamt of so many years past."

Christening his island Taprobane, the ancient Greek name for Ceylon, he built an octagonal villa that allowed for verandahs in every direction; a 1930s folly, which, with small gardens extending through the foliage to the overhanging edges, fully occupied the crest of his island. Rooms revolved outward from a grand central space, and the whole resolved in as open a plan as possible, to allow the flow of space and air. With verandahs spilling out to embrace the landscaped garden and stepped terraces hovering over the ocean, one has the sensation there of living on a landscaped cruise boat.

By embracing the climate and verdant surroundings in Taprobane, the count helped pioneer an indoor-outdoor approach to tropical house design that Europeans, arriving in the tropics with no previous experience in outdoor living, usually approached with great trepidation.

After the count died in the late '40s, Taprobane continued to attract new generations of romantics. The American writer Paul Bowles lived here for many years, alternating seasonally with his better-known home in Morocco.

LEFT The lofty central, octagonal living room (top). A large verandah (middle) extends out onto an open terrace, placed for greeting visitors as well as for watching sunsets over the bay. The master bedroom (bottom) with a traditional canopied bed; windows and French doors open onto private terraces, the jungly garden, and the view. OPPOSITE The loggia, arrived at directly from the central living room, offers a glimpse of garden and ocean beyond.

L U N U G A N G A

ARCHITECT GEOFFREY BAWA

PERHAPS THE MOST MAGICAL GARDEN retreat in the world, Lunuganga was created by the celebrated Sri Lankan architect Geoffrey Bawa as a refuge from his law practice in Colombo (architecture was a later career). Occupying a promontory in a lake near Sir Lanka's west coast, it is set into a landscape of gently rolling hills. Bawa bought the land in 1948 and spent the next forty years clearing and planting, developing a series of orchestrated vistas on an estate that has become a destination for landscape aficionados from all over the world. In its earliest days cinnamon was grown here. When Bawa found the property, it was an abandoned and overgrown rubber plantation. From an existing cottage—since replaced by Lunuganga's main house—on an elevated plateau, Bawa saw promise in a glimpse of a lagoon, as well as the pointed *dagoba* of a distant Buddhist temple, through the dense undergrowth. "The jungle vegetation of the southern hills," Bawa later wrote, "seemed almost impenetrable. Porcupine, mongoose and an occasional cobra lived in it—but one preferred to imagine leopards and centaurs—and there would have to be a clearing cut through if the lake and temple were to be seen from the house."

LEFT The Lunuganga gardens are a sequence of subtly orchestrated experiences. This lower terrace is planted with rice and overhung with trees populated with kingfishers. A neoclassical statue above stands at the end of the upper lawn, facing the main house, which is just out of view.

Bawa set to work clearing and opening up vistas to the water and the temple on a hillcrest beyond. The house and various outbuildings followed, and these became a laboratory for Bawa's experiments as an architect. The house sits perfectly in the landscape, and from it the garden flows organically in all directions. An entry terrace enjoys the morning light and the view described above, which unfolds stage by stage. In the middle distance a sacred Moonamal tree sits on a rise known as Cinnamon Hill, with a Chinese urn from the Ming period artfully placed next to its base. This acts as a resting place for the eye at midpoint between the viewer and the distant lake.

The gardens are arranged around the property as a series of events and visual surprises. A woodland walk brings one to a clearing with a well, a small pond, a cluster of palms, and a series of black glazed Ming pots. This is the Field of Jars. Progressing farther, one arrives at an extended terrace of rice fields edged by a long stone parapet: We are at the edge of the lake. This landscape is punctuated by frangipani trees and the brilliant flight of kingfishers. From here, long flights of stone steps bring one up again to outbuildings and back to the house itself.

The house has a wonderfully languid disposition, with neoclassical overtones stylistically recalling the 1930s. Most furniture in the house and separate studio is from the Dutch period; the more rustic pieces are Portuguese from the seventeenth century.

LEFT A view of the lily pond on the lower terrace (top). The lower terrace (middle) seen from the main house, showing the rice paddy, the stone balustrade, and a corner of the lake. Afternoons are spent in this loggia (bottom), which faces the sunset and the lake. It is shaded by an ancient frangipani. OPPOSITE A pleasing conjunction of steps leads to the main house and studio.

JAVA IS SET IN THE MIDST OF a broad necklace of volcanic islands that form the Nusantara, the Southeast Asian archipelago. Long, narrow, and densely populated, it represents, together with the neighboring island of Bali, the cultural heartland of Indonesia.

For two thousand years, Java, rich in gems, gold, spices, and other prized commodities, and strategically placed on the trade routes linking the Middle East, India, and China, has benefited from a variety of cultural and religious influences. Hindu temples appeared in Java during the seventh century, culminating in the majestic spires of Prambanan, outside Jogjakarta in the middle of the island. For the next two centuries, there was a flourishing of art and literature, and the world's largest Buddhist monument, Borobudur, became a focus for religious and scholarly pilgrimages from China.

The benign and culturally important Majapahit kingdom, established in the thirteenth century, brought an era of stability to the entire archipelago and lasted for two centuries. Its architectural influences—including the structural use of brick walls, gateways, and particular decorative flourishes—are still felt, especially in Bali. By the fifteenth century, regional developments, including the increasing influence of Islam, spread from Mughal India and the Middle East and infiltrated the island, which has since and up to the present day been predominantly Muslim.

The Dutch first set foot in Java at the end of the sixteenth century, initially interested only in trading opportunities. Quickly recognizing the region as an important arena of commerce, they began to find ways to consolidate operations—and control foreign competition—

PRECEDING PAGES Detail of an eighteenth-century Javanese screen (left), rescued from the old Governor's Palace of Batavia (now Jakarta), now on display in the city's excellent Fatahillah Museum. The latter, with its collections of Javanese and Dutch Colonial furniture, was the original city hall, built in the Dutch Colonial style in the seventeenth century. A suite in the Dharmawangsa Hotel in Jakarta (right), designed by Jaya Ibrahim, refreshingly explores regional design references rather than those of Middle America. The decorative canopy is from a Sumatran bridal bed. OPPOSITE Dawn at Borobudur, one of the world's greatest Buddhist monuments. Sitting in the center of a giant valley, it is surrounded by three volcanoes. It is notable particularly for its terraces, ten in all. The first five feature bas-relief depictions of everyday life—images of people, domestic scenes, plenty of interior decorating tips, and house exteriors—as witnessed by Prince Siddhārta on his journey to becoming the Gautama Buddha.

and this led to the formation of the Dutch East India Company with its consequent monopoly of Southeast Asian trade to Europe. Dutch colonization of Java inevitably followed.

This lasted until 1811, at which point the British took over the island for six years, then restored it to the Dutch. This interregnum, though brief, proved influential. The remarkable governor-general, Sir Stamford Raffles, was a scholar and botanist as well as a brilliant diplomat. In addition to initiating important land reforms, which were continued later by the Dutch, and publishing his encyclopedic *History of Java,* which drew international attention to the island's archeological legacy, his influence extended to architecture and design. The neoclassical "Raffles chair," which he introduced, remains a familiar feature of Javanese interiors and hints of the neoclassical architecture that crept into the vocabulary of domestic design.

This influence began a pattern of stylistic assimilation, which has continued ever since and is well described by Peter Schoppert in *Java Style:* "Both European residents and Javanese were linked in a complicity that expressed itself in terms of architecture and design. Javanese and residents both lived in mansions that combined neoclassical elements into a pattern that was essentially Javanese. Although they may have had different tastes and different attitudes, elite Javanese and Europeans, and indeed the wealthy Chinese, lived in a common world." This blend of stylistic elements finds expression today in the work of Javanese designer Jaya Ibrahim.

Most traditional houses in Java are contained within a walled compound. Visitors to houses of substance are greeted in the *pendopo,* an open pavilion whose central area of roof is pitched much more steeply than the outer roof and rises to two points rather than one. This domestic roof profile is distinctively Javanese.

Raffles much admired Java's exotic tropical landscapes, writing that they "may be reckoned amongst the most romantic and highly diversified in the world; uniting all the rich and magnificent scenery, which waving forests, never-failing streams and constant verdure can present, heightened by pure atmosphere and the glowing tints of a tropical sun." This abundance of greenery formed—and still does—an agreeable background to life in Java. Raffles added that its villages are "completely screened from the rays of a scorching sun, and buried amid the foliage of a luxuriant vegetation." Not for nothing was Java often referred to by Europeans as the "Garden of the East."

CINERE

DESIGNER JAYA IBRAHIM

JAYA IBRAHIM DESIGNED THIS HOUSE IN THE suburb of Cinere, on the outskirts of Jakarta, for his parents. Ibrahim studied economics in London, then became an interior designer. Through the '80s he worked for Anoushka Hempel in her London studio, and it was during this period that he designed the Cinere house. The assignment of designing a contemporary house in Jakarta gave Jaya a fresh understanding of his Javanese-Islamic roots and led to the realization that even while working in London, his inspiration was coming from Indonesia. Consequently he decided to open his own design studio in Jakarta and focus on creating design idioms appropriate for Indonesia at the end of the twentieth century.

The house is eclectic, with echoes of Lutyens and even of early Frank Lloyd Wright (seen in the widespread eaves), with a strong underpinning of Indo-European traditions. It owes little, however, to its neighbors, which exhibit the rootlessness of contemporary Indonesian design and its potpourri of Chinese-modern and slick Western styles.

Jaya's interiors display a studied formality: The

LEFT The dining room at Cinere. Jaya placed rows of prints in formalized patterns on almost every wall in the house. This rhythm is repeated on a smaller scale in the dentil ceiling moldings. Ibrahim also designed the tables and chairs.

impression is that of a house belonging to a rarefied nineteenth-century gentleman who is an aesthete and collector. Eighteenth- and nineteenth-century English prints are displayed in friezelike rows, and accumulations of celadon pottery and rare china are lovingly grouped like botanical specimens. Door openings are overscaled and imposing. The high ceilings are delineated by moldings patterned with rectangular ventilation holes. The decoration and the architecture are so closely orchestrated as to seem inseparable.

The house was sold to Mark and Mary Edelson, Americans working in Jakarta. When they decided to buy the house, they asked whether they could have the furnishings too. Jaya's mother, who was to move into the new house that Jaya was designing in the country, agreed, and so the house has kept its homogeneity.

LEFT AND ABOVE An atmosphere of serenity infuses the living room. Framed prints and teak furniture give a sense of continuity between rooms. A long couch faces the garden and is anchored by Sumatran lanterns hung from taffeta swags.

PRECEDING PAGES A hallway (left) looking through to the kitchen. Floor-to-ceiling cupboards exaggerate the verticality of the spaces and create a feeling of luxury. A seating arrangement in a downstairs alcove (right), with a Jaya-designed neoclassical couch, is an exercise in greens and reds. ABOVE LEFT The master bedroom is a lofty, serene space with views of the garden. LEFT A grouping of frogs and other small figures on a shelf in the study. The many prints in the house were taken from sets in books and then mounted. OPPOSITE Braziers light the way for dinner in the garden. The brick-and-concrete house design is eclectic, borrowing from Dutch Colonial, Frank Lloyd Wright's Prairie houses, and Lutyens.

CIPICONG

DESIGNER JAYA IBRAHIM

CIPICONG, IBRAHIM'S ROMANTIC RETREAT in central Java, is first glimpsed across the rice paddies that surround the house, an Asian version of a Palladian villa. Behind the house looms the volcanic profile of Gunung Salek, adding to Cipicong's air of exoticism. The house is near Bogor, which the Dutch developed as a mountain resort. With its famous botanical gardens, it was a popular refuge from the stifling heat of Batavia.

As romantic as its location, Cipicong's genesis is a story in itself. Jaya, while in London during the 1980s as a designer with Anoushka Hempel, narrowly missed winning a nineteenth-century painting of Gunung Salek at a Christie's auction. Regardless of that, he fell in love with the image of the mountain in its rice-field setting. Returning to Java later, and searching for a site for a new house for his mother (and where he and his partner, John Saunders, could spend weekends), Jaya succeeded in finding a site that exactly matched his memory of the painting. Here he built Cipicong,

LEFT Facing an extensive front lawn planted with palms and surrounded by paddy fields, the traditionally Javanese front elevation of Cipicong, with its imposing *pendopo* (entry porch) to greet visitors. OVERLEAF A Venetian balcony with trefoil arches (left), outside Jaya's study, frames an idyllic view of rice fields and reflecting pool. The nineteenth-century lantern originally hung in a mosque. The Grand Canal comes to the rice fields (right): the east elevation with Venetian balcony and reflecting pool. Jaya-designed platforms derived from traditional Javanese seating are drawn up by the pool.

which varies the theme delineated at Cinere: this time a gentleman-aesthete's rural retreat.

Romantic as it is, Cipicong represents Jaya's blueprint for practical living in the tropics. Blending inspiration from a variety of sources—Venetian, Moorish, Palladian, and Javanese—he has created a comfortably cool, well-ventilated house. An internal courtyard promotes airflow, and the polished cement floors are cool underfoot.

Cipicong's north-facing entrance is grand. Visitors arrive at a colonnaded *pendopo:* a traditional Javanese welcoming verandah. Its comfortable seating area also makes it a favorite location to take cocktails and watch the sunset. Beyond this is the dining room, which leads in turn to the colonnaded courtyard. The long south facade, with its continuous verandah, faces the volcano and the morning sun, and this is where breakfast and lunch are usually served. Bedrooms, except the master suite, are placed between this verandah and the courtyard, so that air can flow through between them.

The eastern end of Cipicong—occupied by Jaya's bedroom and study—presents a Venetian facade to the landscape. In front of this, a long reflecting pool extends out into the paddies—a surreal conjunction: rural Java meets the Grand Canal.

Jaya's role as a designer has been to introduce a vocabulary of contemporary design and architecture that is appropriate for a region where little exists. His neo-Orientalist (and Indo-European) vision—which seems to embrace everything east of Venice—offers romantic but nonetheless rational ideas for giving Indonesian design an identity of its own.

LEFT Jaya designed the chairs and cabinets in the dining room (top). A Javanese lantern is suspended over the table. Cement floors are stained with a batik pattern. A cabinet filled with a family collection of blue Dutch china (middle) rests against a wall lined with prints. In the study (bottom) Sumatran celadon pots are grouped on a nineteenth-century Javanese *kas*. OPPOSITE The *pendopo* is the traditional Javanese space for receiving guests. Jaya designed the furniture and also the glazed screen, with heraldic scroll, to block drafts.

PRECEDING PAGES The back loggia (left), with the breakfast table, faces Gunung Salek. A platter of passion fruit for breakfast (right). LEFT Jaya designed the house to revolve around a central courtyard filled with palms, pebbles, and rows of small scallop-edged pots. This space helps circulation from one part of the house to another and promotes the movement of air. TOP A small family room opens onto the central courtyard. ABOVE The courtyard at night, illuminated with candles placed in the rows of pots.

103

OPPOSITE The romantic master bedroom, decorated to evoke a vision of the Orient. Four eighteenth-century Javanese doors screen the bed. ABOVE RIGHT An arrangement of antique bottles rests on a cabinet in the master bedroom. RIGHT In the guest bedroom, a side table displays a family collection of Dutch china, Javanese terra-cotta, and items from the Majapahit period, backed by a Javanese glass painting.

BALI

BALI IS THE MOST EXOTIC OF TROPICAL islands, combining the "oriental mystery of Shangri-La and the romanticism of Gauguin's Tahiti," says writer (and Balinese resident) Bruce Carpenter, "with the promise of the Garden of Eden." To the visitor, it continues to present a unique tapestry of architecture, design, and religious ceremony, interwoven with the island's natural beauty. Its biggest attraction however is the expression of its religion through the everyday life of the Balinese. The decorated temples, the processions, the dance, the spectacular cremations—all of these are part of a continuous living pageant dedicated to the gods. These remarkable devotions are the island's great attraction, rather than its spectacular beaches or scenic beauty. For those you can go to Hawaii or Tahiti.

The religion to which the Balinese are so devoted is Hinduism with an overlay of animism—the worship of Earth and nature. Their one god, Siwa, is manifested through myriad lesser deities worshipped at more than 20,000 temples on the island, plus a multitude of altars and shrines at crossroads, markets, prominent trees, lakes, and rice fields, as well as countless household shrines. Offerings, each attractively handmade of food and flowers woven together with grass, are produced daily to place carefully in most of these holy places. Each Balinese has ties to several temples and shares their upkeep, together with their preparation for festivals: This is the time when these otherwise dormant structures are elaborately decorated for visitation from the gods.

PRECEDING PAGES The hidden valley of Gunung Kawi near Ubud is one of one of Bali's best surprises: apart from ravishing views of rice fields, waterfalls, and an attractive temple (page 106), there are spectacular eleventh-century *candis* (memorials to deified royalty) carved out of the cliffs, which edge the valley floor. Sunrise at a Four Seasons villa at Jimbaran (page 107). The Lotus Pond in Ubud (page 109), with the temple facade beyond, framed by sacred frangipani trees. OPPOSITE The entry courtyard of the Dion residence near Ubud, with its mossy patina. The thatched garden lantern is by Made Wijaya. TOP In the back garden of the same house a statue of Ganesh, the elephant god, is inset in the rear wall. A cat sits in contemplation on the stone ledge over the rock-edged swimming pool. ABOVE A pathway through miniature rice pastures winds past eleventh-century Buddhist monastic caves. These, together with much larger *candis,* line the hidden valley of Gunung Kawi.

Bali has long had an attraction for the creative and the adventurous. With the beginnings of Dutch colonization in the nineteenth century, scholars wrote the first monographs on the culture of Bali. Later, in the 1920s—while still an isolated feudal island—it was visited mainly by anthropologists, musicologists, and filmmakers captivated by the lifestyle of the Balinese. In 1929 the remote island made its debut in the Western world through a series of documentary films, inspiring an elite circle of travelers and celebrities to adopt Bali as their isle at the rainbow's end. Among these were Anaïs Nin, Barbara Hutton, Charlie Chaplin, and Noël Coward, who complained (in verse to Chaplin):

As I was saying this morning to Charlie,
There's far too much music in Bali.
And though as a place it's entrancing,
There's also, I thought, too much dancing.

It seems that each Balinese native
From the womb to the tomb is creative.
And though the results are quite clever,
There's too much creative endeavour!

In the 1930s some of these visitors began to settle: Belgian artist Adrian Le Mayeur de Merpres established himself by the ocean in Sanur, his garden filled with statuary; and the painter Walter Spies arrived from Java and built a several-story bamboo house in the hills near Ubud. Later, wishing to escape from the stream of notables who were increasingly using his house as a way station—including Chaplin and Coward, anthropologists Margaret Mead and Gregory Bateson, Lady Diana Cooper, Doris Duke, Leopold Stokowski, and musicologist Colin McPhee—he fled eastward to build a little house in the village of Iseh, with an unparalleled view of the island's major volcano—and seat of the Balinese gods—Gunung Agung. "I sold my Leica to Jane McPhee," he wrote to his mother, "and with the money I've built a little atelier in the mountains of East Bali, as far as I can go, so it won't be easy to find me." These pioneering dream houses were the prototypes for future expatriate forays into the Balinese landscape.

It was in the 1960s that vacation houses began to appear on the island, which jet travel had made relatively accessible. Borrowing from Balinese vernacular, these were built as open-sided pavilions set in an ideal landscape and furnished with cheerful Balinese fabrics and decorations, bamboo, and colonial furniture. In the last two decades these houses have become progressively more sophisticated and stylish.

The traditional Balinese house is perceived as a living organism. Its design ordained by complex and ancient building codes, it resembles a human being: The head is the ancestral shrine; the arms are the sleeping quarters and living room. Legs and feet are the kitchen and rice granaries. Each of these rooms is a separate building with its own thatched roof, set in a landscaped garden and surrounded by a high wall, creating a compound large enough for an extended family.

Bali's last cultural invasion was more than five hundred years ago, when Hindu influences from India filtered through from Java and transformed the island's religion and architecture. Now the island is in the throes of another upheaval as Western technology, social values, and tourism threaten to overwhelm the island's traditional culture.

The new Bali is already an island transformed. While the Balinese struggle to retain their traditional values, their island is increasingly colonized by tourism. When the Amandari Hotel near Ubud opened in the late 1980s—the first of a series of Aman hotels to be built in Indonesia, it was modeled on indigenous housing and set new standards for boutique hotels (it is still often voted "world's best small hotel" by American travel magazines)—the local Balinese were astonished that Westerners would pay hundreds of dollars a night to stay in a thatched villa. Despite their deceptively simple indigenous appearance, however, the Amandari villas contained almost every luxury known to man (including the refreshing absence of television). The Amandari was followed by other Aman properties: the Four Seasons at Jimbaran Bay, and, grandest of all, the new Begawan Giri, all offering visitors an idealized experience in tropical living, in open pavilions under a thatched roof.

PRECEDING PAGES The verandah of the Angela Vestey residence in southern Bali (left) faces the garden, pool, and small pavilion, with a peaceful landscape of rice fields beyond. A terra-cotta pot (right) serves as a fountain at the Four Seasons resort at Jimbaran Bay. The landscaping is by Made Wijaya. OPPOSITE A sacred bathing pool at Tampak Siring, the eleventh-century water palace near Ubud.

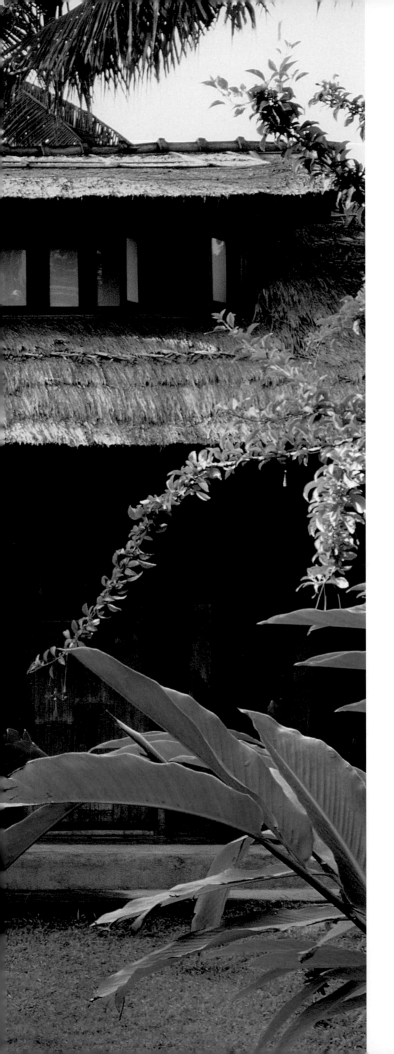

THE BAMBOO HOUSE

DESIGNER PUTU SUARSA

DESPITE ITS PROXIMITY TO THE POPULAR resort of Sanur on the south coast of Bali, the village of Sidakarya is off the beaten track. There is little to bring tourists out along the narrow road, raised due to occasional flooding, that threads its way across the rice fields between Sidakarya and the main coastal highway. The few Westerners who do make an appearance are usually friends of Putu Suarsa en route to pay a visit to his remarkable Bamboo House.

Putu Suarsa is a Balinese designer in his forties, who, when he built the house, lived with his wife and family (including a multitude of aunts, grannies, parents, nephews, cousins, and nieces) in their traditional family compound in the village. He was able to afford the luxury, unusual for a Balinese, of a second house, which he designed not only to entertain friends, but also as a show-place for his design work.

Built in the early 1980s, the Bamboo House remains one of the most innovative houses on the island. It adjoins the workshop and studio for

LEFT The entry courtyard of the Bamboo House near Sanur, its exterior resembling a tropical version of the Cotswolds. Visitors are welcomed by a pot of flowering lotus and a garden filled with ginger and frangipani.

117

ABOVE LEFT The open-sided living room at the Bamboo House, furnished with rattan plantation chair and bamboo couch. Guest suites occupy both ends of the space. LEFT An Indonesian deer figure stands on top of a Javanese chest of drawers; the wall is of slatted bamboo. OPPOSITE The opposing view of the living space. Bamboo blinds, at left, can be lowered during storms. The entrance to a guest suite at the end was designed by Suarsa to resemble a traditional Balinese house facade.

Suarsa's company, Total Design, which produces and sells bamboo furniture (he was one of the first to do so). This is on family land at the edge of the village, and is surrounded by rice fields, bamboo groves, the village soccer field, and a river.

Most afternoons, when work is finished for the day, Suarsa's friends, including landscapist Made Wijaya, whose own Villa Bebek is only ten minutes away, gather under the broad thatched roof of the Bamboo House to gossip, play chess, drink wine, and listen to the twilight chorus of frogs emanating from the courtyard.

Perhaps due to Suarsa's frequent contact with visitors involved in design, fashion, and architecture, the layout of the Bamboo House follows a Western pattern: Everything, except the kitchen, is placed under one roof. The house is approached through a gateway where an inscrutable Sumatran monkey does concierge duty. Inside, there is a courtyard landscaped with alpinia and frangipani; a lotus grows from a terra-cotta indigo-dipping vat. With its roof of deep thatch and its tiny dormers, the L-shaped house could almost be in the Cotswolds, except for the absence of walls.

Under this enveloping roof are living quarters, with guest suites at each end, one of which is placed behind a traditional stone and brick facade. Its bathroom extends beyond the edge of the roof, so that showers can be taken amidst vegetation under the blue sky.

At the other end of building are more guest rooms, this time with an upstairs bedroom featuring a neatly articulated sitting alcove of bamboo built

OPPOSITE The versatility of bamboo: Suarsa-designed furniture, woven wall panels, screen, and blinds—all framed by bamboo columns and roof. TOP A close-up view of roof detailing. ABOVE A sleeping platform is squeezed into the rafters in one of the guest suites.

121

over a study space. The living area is protected by a bamboo wall perforated with large openings, shielding the interior from prevailing winds. It is furnished with Suarsa's own luxurious bamboo couches with cushions of plain canvas. Roll-down bamboo blinds screen the living area from the courtyard during storms.

At the time of its photographing, the house was shared with Takashi Inaba, a Japanese hotelier, who collects antiques and primitive art from all over the Indonesian archipelago. Inaba's constantly changing discoveries sit comfortably with Suarsa's sophisticated use of bamboo—which was unprecedented at the time of its construction on such a large architectural scale. The result is a house that successfully blends tradition with a Westernized sense of innovative design.

LEFT In this wall detail (top), a green edging treatment is used to accent the framing of an opening. An antique teapot sits on a low bamboo-slatted table in the living room (middle). Freshly cut black bamboo used for furniture making (bottom) stands ready outside Suarsa's studio. OPPOSITE An antique Indonesian bamboo ladder and wood carving from Toraja rest against a split-bamboo wall.

PANCHORAN

DESIGNER AND ENVIRONMENTALIST LINDA Garland lives in Panchoran ("the Spring"), an ever-evolving thirty-acre estate that was once rice fields in the village of Nu Kuning near Ubud in central Bali. Worried that someone else would build and compromise her view, Garland gradually acquired more and more parcels as they became available. She is now safe—everything in view is hers. Garland has fashioned the land in a variety of ways, which she describes as "large-scale land sculpture." In front of the main living pavilion the land, planted with chest-high alang-alang grass (used for roofing thatch), descends to the river, rising and falling in shapes that Garland likens to "the cleavage of a giant Henry Moore woman." Teams of workers are employed carving reliefs into exposed volcanic rock on a stretch of hillside, ornamental pools in the ex–rice terraces, and a large swimming pool lined with river rocks and fed by natural spring water. Food supplies for Linda's cook (reputed to be the best on the island) are all grown on the property.

LEFT The entry to Linda Garland's main living pavilion at Nu Kuning, edged with a row of Chinese storage jars. OVERLEAF Panchoran resembles a small village. Here a stone path leads from the kitchen, Linda's own bedroom, and guest cottages, toward the bathroom on the left and the three-tiered main building beyond. Young papaya trees line the path.

Over the years Garland has built clusters of bamboo pavilions—to live in, for her two sons and guests, and another series around an entry courtyard for her design studios and the Environmental Bamboo Foundation, which she established to research ways of using and protecting this versatile material. Garland fashioned her living quarters in the usual Balinese manner. The three-tiered living pavilion, its upper floors originally sleeping quarters for her two boys, is the central focal point, and there are separate structures nearby for cooking, bathing, eating, and sleeping. Her latest project, in a new stylistic direction that she describes as "tribal," adds a new wing to the living pavilion and is developed from Garland's recent designs for a resort in Sumba.

LEFT A decorative rice barn (top) from Sumatra sits on a terrace overlooking the river. An open-air bathroom at Panchoran (middle), its wall lined with river rocks, is built into the slope of the hill. Central columns in the main living pavilion, with Indonesian figures (bottom). OPPOSITE Garland's open-sided master bedroom enjoys a palm-fringed view of her estate. She designed everything in the room: the Dutch Colonial–style chair, cushions, bamboo table, and umbrella holder, as well as the rattan matting on the floor. This bedroom pavilion is constructed entirely of bamboo.

ABOVE LEFT Garland commissioned these traditional rock
carvings in a quiet corner of the estate. LEFT A Garland-
designed bamboo guest house. The circular bamboo containers
hanging from the facade are for sifting rice. OPPOSITE The
view from the terrace of the main pavilion, looking down grassy
slopes toward the river. The vase in the foreground is made
from an exotic form of bamboo.

VILLA BEBEK

DESIGNER MADE WIJAYA

IT IS MORNING AT THE VILLA BEBEK, LANDscapist Made Wijaya's home-and-studio compound set behind high stone walls in a quiet lane on the fringes of Sanur. Waves can be heard breaking on the distant reef, and the sky is patterned with the fronds of countless palms, for the neighborhood was once a coconut plantation. The Villa Bebek (*bebek* is Indonesian for "duck")—a maze of pavilions, courtyards, screening walls, and ornamental ponds—is already busy with gardeners, household staff, and draftsmen going about their business. In the midst of this activity a woman in formal Balinese dress places offerings at auspicious locations in the gardens, while sleepy house guests make their way to a poolside breakfast table. Last but not least, the stentorian voice of Wijaya himself can be heard delivering instructions to assistants and secretaries, while preparing to receive delegations of clients from Singapore and Jakarta.

Australian-born Wijaya visited Bali as an architecture student fresh from Sydney University in the early 1970s and stayed. His career in landscaping was established with the botanical gardens he designed for the Bali Hyatt in Sanur, and blossomed further with his gardens for the Amandari Hotel and the Four Seasons in Jimbaran Bay.

LEFT A guest bedroom at the Villa Bebek, inspired by a visit to Morocco, with a Balinese canopied bed. The figure in the niche is of Berber soapstone.

Meanwhile, his "Stranger in Paradise" column in a Balinese newspaper (since published as a book) covered events ranging from the doings of café society to temple festivals. These essays opened a new chapter in the discourse on the island's unique social and cultural life—following in the footsteps of luminaries like artist Miguel Covarrubias and anthropologists like Margaret Mead. What gives Wijaya's luminous and often hilarious journal its unique credibility is that he is the only outside commentator on Balinese life and ritual who has understood every word of what is transpiring: In addition to Kawi, the language of the high priests, he speaks the three Balinese languages fluently.

Wijaya is also an authority on the history of Balinese architecture, and the Villa Bebek, which he designed and built in 1990, is a unique laboratory for living and working in the tropics. Within the compact dimensions of this walled compound, which was architecturally inspired by the blending of colonial and traditional styles found in Balinese palaces, are nine pavilions housing design studios, offices, kitchens, residential quarters for Wijaya, and guest cottages. Each of these open onto garden terraces on at least two sides. The harmonious knitting of the various activities within the limited space is what makes the Villa Bebek a success, and it is all done with landscaping. An interweaving of courtyards, walls punctuated with a variety of Balinese gateway openings, ornamental pools, strategically placed shade trees, hedges, decorative planting, and paving provide a rich variety of visual experiences. Yet where it is needed, privacy can be found.

OPPOSITE Framed by frangipani, fishtail palms, and bougainvillea, the pool is bordered by the breakfast terrace (to the right). The undulating stripes in the pool are an homage to David Hockney. RIGHT The poolside breakfast terrace (top), overhung with flowering vines. A Wijaya-designed garden lantern (middle) next to a Moroccan-blue wall. The staff terrace next to the entrance (bottom). The compound walls are painted blue using powdered pigment from Morocco.

TOP A spray of baby coconuts decorates a tabletop in the main courtyard. ABOVE Looking into the main courtyard: Paving stones lead toward a guest bedroom suite, the open-air pavilion on the upper floor, and design studios to the right. RIGHT The main courtyard looking across to the guest bedroom suite on the upper level. The vertical tablets are five-hundred-year-old boundary stones from the island of Sumba; the small statues are from Sumbawa.

PRECEDING PAGES A verandah (left) overlooking a garden courtyard, with a 1930s Javanese table and chairs by Jaya Ibrahim. An indoor dining room (right), decorated with antique Javanese Wayang Kulit shadow puppets. The husband and wife figures framed in the doorway are also Javanese.
LEFT The upper-floor guest bedroom is open on all sides, surrounded by a balustrade and a view of the treetops. The lace netting is suspended from a bamboo-framed panel, which is in turn suspended from the ceiling. Presiding *legong* dance figures are Balinese. The lamps incorporate Chinese pots and were designed by Wijaya. ABOVE The paved courtyard garden with ornamental pond and luxuriant landscaping. A guest cottage is in the background.

ABOVE LEFT A corner of the garden, with miniature frangipani and a Wijaya-designed stone fountain set against a stone garden wall. LEFT The courtyard garden, with its fish pond and stepping-stones. The building on the left is a guest house.
OPPOSITE The furniture in the upstairs living room is an eclectic mix. The figure of a woman on the table is Javanese. The upper-floor guest bedroom can be seen across the courtyard to the left.

VILLA AGNES, TAMAN BEBEK

DESIGNER MADE WIJAYA

A MILE DOWNSTREAM FROM THE AMANDARI Hotel, near Ubud, the Ayung River courses its way through a deep, steep-sided ravine. Below the village of Sayan it describes a tight S curve, and the ridge above is one of the most celebrated views in Bali. In pride of place (and on the site of musicologist Colin McPhee's house in the 1930s) Made Wijaya built first a house for himself, and then several others as guest cottages. These are now grouped together as the Taman Bebek Hotel and are distinguished by Wijaya's lush landscaping, pools, and sinuous pathways, giving each one a sense of privacy and romance.

The Villa Agnes, built originally for a French friend, resembles an Australian bungalow, with everything under one roof. Verandahs extend around the perimeter, raised so that occupants can gaze out though the tropical foliage to the ravine beyond.

LEFT The colorful dining room at the Villa Agnes, with the kitchen in the background. The window openings frame a vista of dense jungle.

145

The villa was designed with an outer zone: a verandah that wraps around an inner, enclosed bedroom sanctuary. Rows of shuttered French doors can be shut tight in bad weather and thrown open again when the sun reappears. The tiered thatched roof allows hot air to escape through high-level vents, creating a natural cooling system for the interior. The kitchen is large and airy, with a dining table and views through large windows into the trees. The bathroom shares space with a tiny garden that projects out beyond the roof eaves.

Villa Agnes is the perfect small tropical house, adapting easily to sudden weather changes and providing an easy interplay between both indoors and outdoors, and public and private areas.

LEFT The verandah overlooks a picturesque garden and lily pond (top). A still life (middle) of a partially opened durian fruit, Javanese figures of a man and wife, and a heraldic glass painting, from Java. The entry porch (bottom) with bamboo armchair. OPPOSITE Here the entry porch is glimpsed through tropical landscaping.

OPPOSITE This bathroom at Villa Agnes has its own enclosed garden, protected by a high wall. ABOVE RIGHT The comfortably furnished verandah, which wraps around on two sides, enjoys an elevated view of the garden. French doors lead into the bedroom. RIGHT The bedroom, with French doors. Beside this is an altar. The roof space is ventilated, helping to keep the interior cool. The bathroom is through the curtain to the right.

AMIR RABIK'S COMPOUND

THE MAIN ROAD WINDS OUT OF UBUD, THE popular mountain community, and heads toward the village of Penesekan. A small driveway hidden in a grove of trees leads to a set of enigmatic bamboo gates. Inside is an extensive array of bamboo pavilions, the home and workplace of designer Amir Rabik.

Born on the nearby island of Madura, Rabik brings a lifelong experience of the tropics to bear on his residential design work and his choice of materials. His bedrooms are placed on upper levels to catch all the breezes from a deep ravine, which his property overlooks. The lower living areas are kept as open as possible, with majestic views of the surrounding slopes, and filled with comfortable pillows arranged as seating.

The most frequented space in his entire compound, however, is his outdoor dining room on a nearby terrace. Here he entertains a wide range of guests in great style, from English rock stars to

LEFT Sunrise on the front verandah of the original cottage on Amir Rabik's property, built in the 1960s. The couch is Javanese. Below the verandah is a fish pond and an extensive garden.

151

Buddhist priests on their way from Seattle to visit the Dalai Lama. Trees provide the roof canopy and crickets and frogs the ambiance as dinner is served on Rabik's long, beautifully laid table set with plates, napkins, and objects found in local villages.

Guests relax first in a small thatched pavilion filled with giant pillows where Rabik serves drinks and hors d'oeuvres presented on elegant platters. On special nights the frangipani tree next to this pavilion is festooned with oil lamps made from coconut shells, and a gamelan orchestra and dance troupe from the village provides entertainment.

Rabik first discovered this corner of Ubud in the mid-1980s with his ex-wife, environmentalist and designer Linda Garland. Together they transformed a run-down vacation house into a comfortable family home to raise their two sons, Liam and Arif.

When Garland moved to her nearby thirty-acre property, Rabik designed more pavilions to accommodate his fast-growing design business. Consequently the compound has come to resemble a small village. Rabik's tropical gardens extend around each structure and echo with the sounds of craftsmen busy working on projects destined for clients around the world.

LEFT Rabik designed this large *bale* (pavilion) in the garden (top) for relaxing and for parties. Lamps made from coconut shells are hung from the branches of a frangipani tree for a party (middle). The terraced slopes (bottom) are set with a Chinese storage jar. OPPOSITE Another Rabik-designed pavilion. This is also used for entertaining and as a guest house.

OPPOSITE Rabik is noted for his elegant entertaining and has set the dining table for lunch with lotus leaves as place settings. On the wall beyond are Javanese clay figures set on stone supports. ABOVE RIGHT Rabik designed this garden gateway, made of local brick. RIGHT The facade of the original brick-built cottage, with steps leading to the garden.

ABOVE LEFT The master bedroom has an elaborate Chinese bed. The Rabik-designed table in the foreground is made of coconut wood. LEFT This detail shows an antique Javanese fabric support for a canopied bed in the guest bedroom. OPPOSITE A Tau-Tau ancestral portrait figure from Toraja graces a guest bedroom.

THE HARDY
RESIDENCE

ARCHITECT CHEONG YEW KUAN

IN 1989, JEWELRY DESIGNER JOHN HARDY and his wife and business partner, Cynthia, found an ideal site for a house on a piece of land over-looking the Ayung River, downstream from the Amandari Hotel near Ubud. They spent several years, before finally starting to build, getting to know the land, staying first in a tent and then in a small pavilion near the precipitous edge of the ravine. Their philosophy, which sprung partly from earlier back-to-nature hippie days, was to create a house as transparent as possible to preserve not only the view of rice paddies and volcanoes, but also the site itself, and its sense of being an open space.

The young Malaysian architect Cheong Yew Kuan had similar conclusions about the site. "When I first walked on the property," he said, "I realized I just could not block the view." In 1993 the Hardys pur-chased several hundred retired ironwood utility poles, each one twenty feet in length, and con-struction began. Yew Kuan developed the concept of using the poles to build the house on stilts,

LEFT The transparent lower floor of the Hardy residence almost resembles a medieval tithed barn. The entrance is across a bridge to the right; stairs are at left. Massive recycled timbers span through the foreground. Structural supports are of recycled ironwood; secondary supports are dead trees from Java. OVERLEAF Rice paddies and the landscape beyond are visible through the house.

159

inspired by photos of multifamily longhouses in Borneo, each several hundred feet long and raised above the ground.

The house Cheong envisaged now straddles the site, raised fifteen feet above the ground. The lower floor is completely open. As visitors enter the garden they do see the house, but simultaneously they see the rice fields and landscape beyond. The concept of transparency was successfully achieved.

Yew Kuan's perspective on Balinese architecture provides a rationale for his design. "In Balinese houses the most important and ornate elements," he says, "are the gates. The typical house has three courtyards on an axis linked by gates. The buildings inside are simple. Progression through a Balinese house is experiential—we are particularly aware of the surrounding walls and the courtyard spaces."

A cobbled courtyard announces the Hardy property. An imposing thatched gate, flanked by mud walls, opens to admit the visitor into a second courtyard (the front garden), which is landscaped simply with grass, a stone path, and trees. The latter conceal the residence until one is quite close, then the vista of the house and distant view is revealed.

Yew Kuan describes the house itself as the second gateway, one that frames the view and the people within. Its narrowness in relation to its length supports his suggestion that it is a massive wall (or gate) across the property. Beyond the house is the back garden—the third courtyard—which is part lawn, part vegetable garden. At one end is a paved area with pool and terrace for outdoor dining and entertaining. At midpoint on the low, undulating

LEFT A corner of the garden (top), with patinated stone urns. The lower-floor seating area (middle) has a view of rice fields. The vegetable garden (bottom) is at the back of the house. OPPOSITE A canvas-and-resin canopy gives storm protection to the mud staircase. This view is from the landing, looking toward the back garden and rice fields.

back wall is a small gate leading to a dramatic spiral staircase that drops eighty feet to Hardy-owned rice fields and the river.

The lower level of the house is open to the garden and is used for dining and entertaining in comfortable seating areas. These can be protected in inclement weather by a vast sailcloth that drops on the side facing the river—and prevailing winds. A central staircase leads to the upper level, where two bedrooms and a large study/living room hover fifteen feet above the ground. The sensation up here is of living in the treetops. These rooms are fitted with huge French doors on both sides, which open to catch the breezes filtering through the trees. When closed they provide for the decadent luxury of air-conditioning when necessary.

The Hardys were helped with decorating decisions by designer Hinke Zieck. Furnishings are mostly Indonesian—the Hardys have long collected antique Javanese and Dutch colonial furniture— mixed with American Arts and Crafts chairs, and rugs from the Caucasus. John Hardy designed light fixtures and bathroom hardware specially for the house, as well as the master bed, which he fashioned from old teak. He also added unobtrusive luxuries such as low-voltage movement-sensor lighting.

With their highly resolved notions on how to live with style and comfort in the tropics, the Hardys, together with Yew Kuan, have developed a house that is "future-rustic": a beguiling combination of high-tech luxuries (much appreciated during the rainy season) together with the rustic, primal qualities of its architecture.

OPPOSITE Furniture in the upstairs sitting room is a mix of Javanese and Dutch Colonial; rugs are from the Caucasus. Hand-beaten brass lamps were made in the Hardy studio. RIGHT A mud corridor used as back entry (top) links the garages and kitchen. Hardy owns these rice fields in the ravine behind his house (middle); the undulating mud walls are of his design. A corner of the kitchen (bottom).

ABOVE LEFT The lavishly scaled master bedroom occupies one end of the upper floor. The Hardy-designed teak bed is draped with unbleached muslin, which is tied back in the day-time. LEFT A carved wood soap stand in the copper-lined shower room, with a bamboo grove outside the window open-ing. OPPOSITE Loofahs hang from simple wooden pegs in the copper-lined shower.

BEGAWAN GIRI

ARCHITECT CHEONG YEW KUAN

BEGAWAN GIRI, A GROUP OF FIVE VILLAS SET in twenty acres of pristine jungle overlooking the Ayung River, is the dream of Bradley Gardner, a British entrepreneur and hotelier. While touring Bali in 1989 with his wife, Debbie, Gardner visited the village of Begawan, near Ubud, and saw the ravishing property with its central promontory hovering over the three-hundred-foot-deep ravine in which the river lies. He immediately bought it and began to buy the adjoining lots until he owned all the land within view of the central area. It was some time before he decided to make the property into a resort.

The early '90s were spent landscaping; in particular, cutting steps down into the ravine. A sacred spring which emerges halfway provided the source for a water garden a few feet above the river level. Here, in a beautiful jungle setting, the springwater drops in a tumultuous cascade and emerges into three cut-rock plunge pools, which are now the focus of the resort's Balinese-style health spa. The Ayung River sweeps majestically just below.

Together with architect Cheong Yew Kuan, Gardner began to plan five large-scale villas. Their early

LEFT The sybaritic water-garden spa in the Tirta Ening villa at Begawan. In the foreground is a conventionally shaped bathtub carved out of a giant rock and fed from a bamboo spout. Pools and jacuzzis beyond are edged by ferns and cascades set in a rocky cliff.

169

decision was to preserve the edge of the Ayung ravine so that nothing could be seen from the water, learning from other visually disruptive resorts elsewhere on the same beautiful river. Consequently the villas are set just below the promontory on the other side and overlook a smaller ravine.

Yew Kuan designed each villa to be thematically distinct and to reflect the architecture and culture of various parts of Indonesia. Each is named after one of the natural elements: fire, wind, water, forest, and earth. Bayugita (Windsong) was built first, an homage to traditional Balinese architecture with echoes of colonial Java. Next to this is Tirta Ening (Clear Water). Here, pavilions of 150-year-old recycled teak float over lily ponds. A minimalist elegance of line helps give this complex a Zen-like feel. Contrasting with this, and next in line, is Tejasuara (Sound of Fire), where Yew Kuan created a tribal, almost Tiki-like ambience. His influence was the island of Sumba, from which Gardner imported 1,200 tons of rugged limestone. The primal feel is reinforced by the use of recycled ironwood telegraph poles, rough-hewn logs, woven bamboo, and palms native to Sumba.

Wanakasa (Forest in the Mist) hangs over the end of the promontory. The sounds of the river can be heard far below; dense mists rise up from the valley in the mornings; and, as it clears, monkeys can sometimes be spotted on the opposite slopes. The last villa is Umabona (House of the Earth Son), influenced by early Majapahit palaces. This is both formal and romantic, set around an inner pool.

With its own poultry, fish, and prawn farms, vegetable gardens and fruit orchards, Begawan is self-contained, an estate in which the traveler can lose himself in a relatively undisturbed natural paradise.

LEFT A villa set in Rousseauesque foliage (top). The spa, fed by a cascading sacred spring, is located at the base of the ravine (middle). The edge of the Wanakasa villa pool (bottom), overlooking the ravine. OPPOSITE A pavilion set in a corner of the Tirta Ening villa's spa and water garden.

THE HOUSE AT ISEH

AT THE EASTERN END OF THE ISLAND, FAR from the tourist bustle of Ubud and Sanur, there is another Bali, serene and little touched by tourism. In the valley of Sideman, overlooked by the majestic profile of Gunung Agung, the mountain village of Iseh still possesses the magic that entranced visitors earlier in the century. On the edge of this village, perched on a high terrace with dramatic views, is the country retreat of Hugo Jereissati.

Wishing to escape the bustle and busy social scene of Sanur, where he lives for part of the year, Jereissati leased this perfect hideaway on the edge of the mountain village of Iseh. From the terrace of this historic little house, resembling a box at the opera, one can sit for days, transfixed by its unparalleled view of rice fields and villages dwarfed by the sacred volcano.

Jereissati follows in the footsteps of artist Walter Spies, who arrived in Iseh in 1937 to escape the flow of celebrities who were using his Ubud studio as a hotel. Falling in love with the picturesque village and surroundings, Spies built the house as his atelier on this shelf of land with one of the best

LEFT The terrace at Iseh, with its famous view of the sacred volcano Gunung Agung, and a cascade of rice fields. The Indian leader Jawaharlal Nehru, who famously described Bali as "the morning of the world," visited this terrace in 1957.

views in Indonesia. When he died in 1942, a Swiss painter, Theo Meier, moved in. Meier lived there until the early 1970s.

In 1963 the volcano erupted with explosive force, a disaster in which thousands of Balinese died. Lava flowed over the rice fields, finally stopping by the river in front of Meier's terrace. The house was eventually rebuilt by Italian writer Idanna Pucci, who lived there until the early '90s, passing it on to Jereissati.

The roads to Iseh are always in a bad state of repair, which is a requisite for all successful retreats—only the intrepid come to visit you. After a bone-jarring ride, the visitor finally negotiates a steep cobbled track up to a tiny plaza with a temple to one side and the entry to the house on the other. Beyond this is the pedestrians-only village.

Inside the entry gate, a covered colonnade brings visitors through to the terrace, passing guest bedrooms on the way, with a glimpse through on the other side to a separate building that Jereissati has renovated and made into his own bedroom and study. The house is simple as befits a retreat with so compelling a view, and it is now decorated with a light, almost Caribbean touch.

Almost every tropical country has one or two magical retreat houses built by idealistic Europeans —artists, writers, or dreamers—always with a wonderful view and often with great simplicity. This is one of the best in Bali. The English writer Anna Mathews, author of *The Night of Purnama,* an account of the 1963 eruption and its aftermath, described the view from the terrace: "Once you have lived in this place you can never be the same again. You are driven mad by beauty."

LEFT Woven cane seating is placed outside on the entry verandah (top). Near a door, a Chinese pot is filled with Balinese umbrellas ready for the next shower (middle). The entry door (bottom) greets visitors arriving from a small, stone-cobbled village plaza. OPPOSITE This door leads from the entry verandah to Jereissati's master suite.

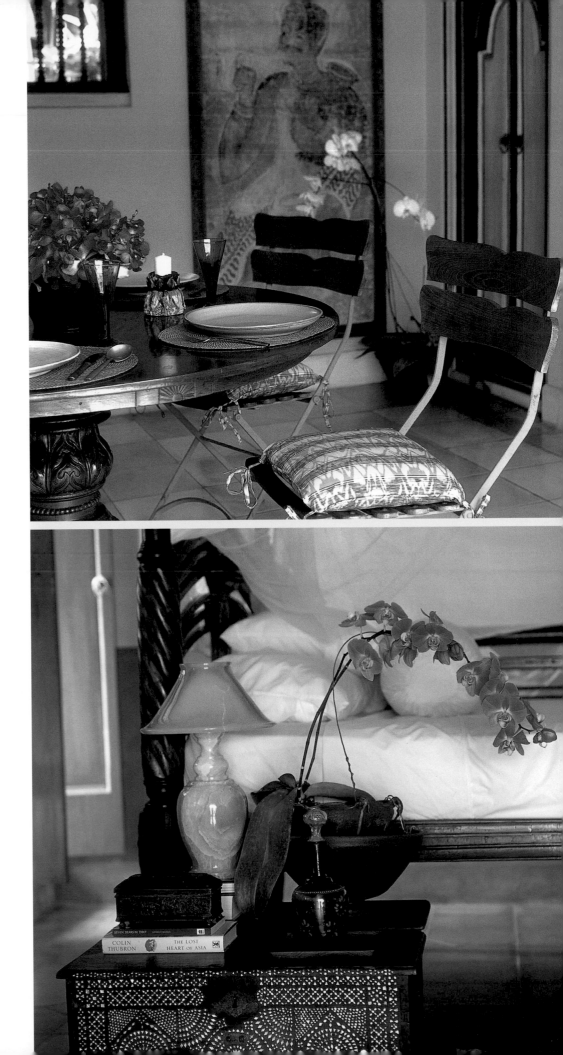

OPPOSITE This romantic guest bedroom is furnished with an antique brass bed. ABOVE RIGHT The dining room. Simple metal chairs have cushions of cotton batik. The painting is of a Balinese prince. The floor is polished cement. RIGHT The master bedroom with its Dutch Colonial–style canopied bed and inlaid Sumatran chest.

MEXICO

AND BELIZE

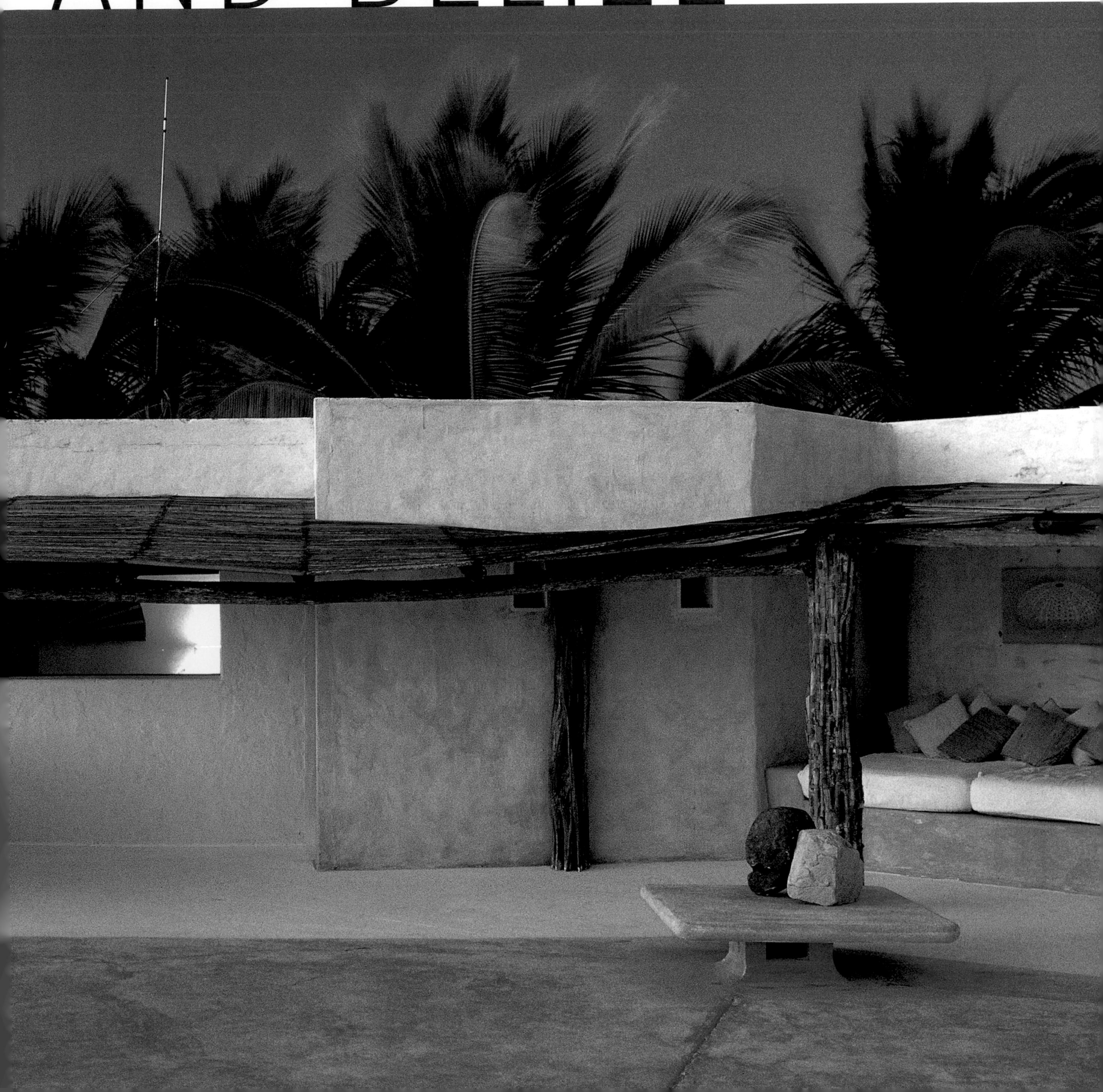

BLESSED WITH MORE THAN 2,000 MILES of sunswept coastline, the Mexican Pacific extends from the dry desert landscapes of Baja California in the north to the states of Chiapas, Oaxaca, and Guerrero in the south, a land of coconut palms, jungle, and tropical humidity. Here, as elsewhere, Mexico is a land of color. The houses on this coast dazzle with brilliant pinks, yellows, and reds, always refreshing after the beige of the United States. Arriving in the village of Careyes, one has the sense of seeing color for the first time.

With their *palapa* roofs and curved walls, houses of the Mexican Pacific have evolved into a signature style that is distinctive and homogenous. Since the region is blessed with a warm climate, it is possible to live outdoors throughout the year, and public spaces are consequently open to the elements. This evolution is a recent one, however, beginning in the late 1970s in the resort of Acapulco. In the preceding two decades, international modernism was the style of choice in this fast-growing resort, as it was elsewhere on the coast. Then, in the mid-seventies, Gloria Guinness and her husband, Loel, visited Acapulco and decided to build a holiday house on a hilltop site overlooking the bay. Searching for inspiration, she noticed the indigenous thatched huts that adorned the local beaches. Hiring Marco Aldaco, a young architect from Guadalajara,

PRECEDING PAGES An indigenous thatched cottage with louvered windows (left) near Merida in the Yucatán. The roof terrace at Casa Mi Ojo in Careyes (right) was inspired by indigenous design. RIGHT Playa Rosa in Careyes harbor. Behind the beach are simple thatched guest cottages and a small restaurant.

she developed with him a new kind of resort house with a thatched *palapa* roof. Together they evolved an architecture without glass, with walls eliminated from the living areas opened to nature. This is architecture arrived at intuitively, emotional rather than cerebral. Intrinsically Mexican, and perfect for the climate and the relaxed lifestyle that the Guinnesses had come here to enjoy, this house became the blueprint for housing along the Mexican Riviera. The international style was henceforth rejected for one based on the simple thatched models that had existed on the coast for centuries.

The thatched roof—*palapa* as it is known in Mexico—proves to be eminently practical. The palm fronds provide excellent insulation: The bleached surface facing the sky has good reflective properties, and the myriad air pockets within prevent the transmission of heat.

One of Aldaco's next clients on the Pacific coast was an Italian, Gianfranco Brignone, who decided to build a house at Costa Careyes, a tiny bay shielded by rocky headlands two hours drive south of Puerto Vallarta. Here, Aldaco repeated the *palapa*-roofed living area, this time supported by exotic-looking tree trunks bound with strangler-fig vine discovered in the local forests (it is said that the contractor brought one in by mistake and was immediately sent off to find more), and with pink-colored walls. As Careyes developed into the sizable resort village of today, the giant *palapa*-roofed living pavilion, with its strangler-vine supports, and the pink-stuccoed massing of the sleeping quarters became a signature style, giving Careyes a sense of architectural homogeneity that is probably unique in twentieth-century coastal developments.

The architects working in Careyes today—Manolo Mestre, Diego Villaseñor, Duccio Ermenegildo, Jean-Claude Galibert, Aldaco, and others—continue the same theme, an architecture that is perfectly tuned to a relaxed, celebratory lifestyle. Similarly inspired houses are also proliferating in Ixtapa, Zihuatanejo, and other resort communities. A few of these are occupied full-time. Most, however, serve as vacation retreats.

Common to these houses is the *palapa,* a grand living space for entertaining. Its lofty, vented interior space and low eaves both contribute to keep its interior cool; its sides are open to the garden and the view. The bedrooms are enclosed in a more conventional way but usually have doors that slide away to open onto private terraces, allowing a choice between inside-outside living or air-conditioned enclosure in wet weather. These Mexican bedrooms (and also the enclosed bathrooms) are less daring than their open-to-nature Balinese counterparts.

OPPOSITE A bird's-eye view of Careyes harbor, with its terraced casitas. TOP The living *palapa* in the influential Casa Guinness in Acapulco. ABOVE The kitchen door of La Meta near Ixtapa. Designed by architect Enrique Zozalla, with help from Duccio Ermenegildo, it is fashioned from local tree stems. OVERLEAF Artist Mari-Carmen Hernandez chose these brightly colored hammocks for La Meta, her house near Ixtapa.

CASA CLARK

ARCHITECT MARCO ALDACO

IN THE LATE 1970S TOM CLARK WAS LOOKING for a site on the Mexican coast to build a house. He discovered Careyes by accident: While fixing a flat tire during a road trip to Acapulco, he was by chance rescued by Giorgio Brignone. As Careyes was at the next turnoff, Clark was invited for an impromptu visit. As do most people when they first glimpse this beautiful place, Clark fell in love. During this visit, he was shown Mi Ojo, Marco Aldaco's recently finished house for Giorgio's father, Gianfranco Brignone, which also made a great impression. At this point he knew he had found his architect and soon after bought a cliff-top site just along from Mi Ojo.

Discussions with Aldaco over a suitable house design culminated in a visit to see the Guinness House in Acapulco, and this became the model for Casa Clark. Consequently, Aldaco designed a round *palapa* for the main living space, surrounded by a tropical garden. Bedrooms and guest quarters occupy separate pavilions next to the main *palapa*. This time, however, Aldaco placed a large pool in front hugging the cliff edge. In a counterpoint to the tranquillity of the house a dramatically located Jacuzzi—built into the rocks below—is reached by precipitous steps down the cliff face.

LEFT The *palapa* living space at Casa Clark, with simple equipal seating, has stuccoed columns supporting the thatched roof. It opens onto the front terrace and pool.

TOP The dramatic jacuzzi, built into the rocks, echoes the swirl of the ocean below. ABOVE The guest cottages, with the Careyes harbor beyond. RIGHT The *palapa* faces a terrace and a wraparound pool.

CASA LA SELVA

ARCHITECT JEAN-CLAUDE GALIBERT

GIORGIO AND ANA BRIGNONE'S NEW HOUSE is set in the steep jungle slopes behind Playa Rosa in the Careyes harbor. La Selva is one of five houses designed by Jean-Claude Galibert as the latest property venture of the company run by Giorgio and his father, Gianfranco Brignone.

Giorgio had long been attracted to the La Selva site, with its picture-perfect views of the harbor, but it was not until the house was nearly finished that he decided to keep it for himself. In doing so he was prompted by a realization that his was now a growing family with a daughter, Juliana, and that the casita they shared—also overlooking the harbor, but with no outdoor space—was really too small.

Some alterations were necessary to adapt the house to their needs, and a small seating area was added at the far end of the pool. It is now perfect for the family.

LEFT The pool terrace at Casa la Selva, off the living *palapa,* with the master bedroom to the left. The house is built into a hillside that overlooks the Playa Rosa and Careyes harbor. Doors on the right open into an air-conditioned media room and library. At the left end of the terrace is a seating area that offers protection from the sun.

ABOVE LEFT A pathway lined with bougainvillea connects guest bedrooms with the pool terrace. LEFT A corner of the living *palapa*. The column is a local tree wrapped with strangler vine. OPPOSITE Quiet seating in a corner of the pool terrace, shaded by wood slats and giant elephant ear plants.

OPPOSITE The pool, with an infinity edge, overlooks the Playa Rosa and Careyes harbor. Casa dos Estrellas can be seen at the top left. ABOVE RIGHT The pool merges with the jungle beyond. RIGHT The pool terrace seen from the living *palapa*.

ABOVE LEFT The table set for dinner in the dining area of the *palapa*. LEFT Carpeted steps lead up to the canopied bed in the master bedroom. OPPOSITE The living *palapa*, with the elevated dining area beyond. The coffee table is from India; columns are local tree trunks covered with strangler vine.

LAS ALAMANDAS

ISABEL GOLDSMITH INHERITED THE NINETY-acre Las Alamandas estate from her grandfather, Antenor Patiño, when he died in 1978. Patiño had major plans for Las Alamandas, intending to create a resort as grand as his earlier creation, Las Hadas in Acapulco. When Goldsmith took over Las Alamandas, situated on a lonely stretch of the Pacific coast and a ninety-minute drive south of Puerto Vallarta, it consisted of an infrastructure of unpaved roads cut into the jungle, a landing strip for small planes, and little else. She fell in love with this remote paradise, with its perfect half-mile-long beach, its lagoons rich in wildlife, and its setting of low hills covered in trees and cactus.

She had no intention, however, of creating a miniature Acapulco. Instead, working with architect Gabriel Orosco, she concentrated on building a small group of villas that friends might visit, an idea that soon evolved into the creation of a small-scale exclusive resort. Using her own interpretation of the vibrant colors of Mexico, Goldsmith created a uniquely festive mood for Las Alamandas, together with an architecture that was unashamedly romantic, and which, small in scale as it was, did little to disturb the fragile environment.

LEFT A pathway leads up from the beach to the original villas, crowned with a small dome. Landscaping is done with indigenous cacti.

OPPOSITE A Mestre-designed bed made with local timber, in the lower floor bedroom. The traditionally Mexican brick vaulted roof is made without support during construction. ABOVE RIGHT The upstairs bedroom. The balcony balustrade echoes the design of the bed downstairs; windows are louvered for ventilation. RIGHT The exterior of the villa designed by Mestre. The broad verandah faces the ocean.

Recently Isabel hired architect Manolo Mestre to help design additional villas, a large *palapa* for entertaining, and miniature *palapacitas* at either end of the pool. Orosco had died, and Mestre was concerned that his new designs should stay in the spirit of the earlier villas. "I wanted to be very respectful," he says, "of the beautiful work he did for Isabel." Las Alamandas now takes its place as one of the world's most romantic getaways.

OPPOSITE Mestre designed this miniature *palapa,* with a raised upholstered platform, to provide poolside shelter. RIGHT A hammock for enjoying the sunset view of the beach (top). Isabel added bright Mexican color to these steps (middle) leading to the villas. A stone dolphin sits on a balustrade (bottom), surrounded by colorful landscaping. OVERLEAF The beach *palapa.* Equipal chairs line the bar to the right. Columns, enwrapped with strangler vine, are from the local forests.

CASA DOS ESTRELLAS

ARCHITECT MANOLO MESTRE

A FESTIVE HOUSE, CASA DOS ESTRELLAS reflects the joie de vivre of its owners, actress (and former James Bond girl) Luciana Paluzzi and her movie-producer husband, Michael Solomon. It straddles a spectacular site on the southern headland of the Careyes harbor, with sweeping 360-degree views of the coastline and numerous islets, the harbor, and the village of Costa Careyes. The cylindrical forms of the house erupt from the hillside, topped by a lookout tower. The idea of the tower was suggested to the architect Manolo Mestre by Michael Solomon, who wanted a place from which to enjoy the extraordinary view and watch the stars.

The property rises vertiginously from the street entry to the living areas at the headland's crest; a cobbled drive flanked between lush groves of bougainvillea deposits visitors at the house itself. A small paved patio flows into an open living area and a partially enclosed dining room. A sculptural circular staircase acts as a focal point and hub for routes through the house to a roofed patio and terraces and pool beyond. The staircase leads upward to the *palapa*-roofed living space and to linked garden terraces, from which pathways continue to the guest suites that cascade down the hillside.

LEFT A large oval pool, with an infinity edge, seems suspended over the Careyes harbor. The yellow house on the far headland is Gianfranco Brignone's Mi Ojo, the first such house to be built in Careyes.

Regarding these suites, Mestre says, "I love the way in the Greek islands the houses are terraced into the cliffs. I arranged each one with its own private terrace, reached by landscaped pathways." The pool is oval for two reasons. As Mestre recalls, "I imagined the pool as a third eye, to look deeper into your soul—a very tantric subliminal message. Also, an oval is never-ending: Your eye follows its outline endlessly, while the infinity edge brings the ocean right up to the pool." Mestre's oval echoes the curvilinear architecture and is designed to fit within the extremities of the garden: A one-hundred-year-old cactus and a small but venerable tree remain undisturbed. The latter hangs over the pool and provides shade from the afternoon sun while the bather contemplates the panorama, as well as squadrons of pterodactyl-like pelicans, gliding silently on the updraft from the lofty cliffs on which the house sits, just below eye level.

Mestre's first idea was for a house "like a village cascading down the hill," he recalls, "but the Solomons wanted a grander house, with formality and symmetry, and then I happened to visit Naples and saw the Castello overlooking the bay with its four turrets, guarding the harbor." Mestre likes "the sensuality of the rounded shapes. From the tower the round shapes below offset the harshness of the landscape, the rocks and the cliffs, playing feminine against masculine. Also the curves are good feng shui. Curves between the floor, the walls, and the ceilings keep the energies flowing. Loel Guinness used to talk about his bedroom, also with the same curvatures: 'There is no place where the eye stops, allowing you to dream as you go to sleep.'"

LEFT Stairs (top) lead up to a guest suite. Casa Dos Estrellas occupies a headland overlooking the harbor (middle). A sun-splashed wall and foliage (bottom). OPPOSITE Steps wind up through a cactus garden, carefully avoiding a venerable one-hundred-year-old specimen.

PRECEDING PAGES The main living *palapa* is primarily
used for entertaining (left). The bar is in the center. Colorful
upholstery in the main living *palapa* (right); through the
opening is a view of the tropical garden. OPPOSITE Mestre
designed the house as a series of cylinders. Each circular
area of the roof terrace is defined by paving patterns and
edged with bougainvillea. ABOVE RIGHT Another seating area
with Mestre-designed benches and a built-in couch; the stairs
lead to the roof terrace and main *palapa*. RIGHT The circular
dining room. These windows can be closed during windy
weather. OVERLEAF A guest bedroom. The use of Mexican
colors is especially strong. Shelves are built in and function
as nightstands.

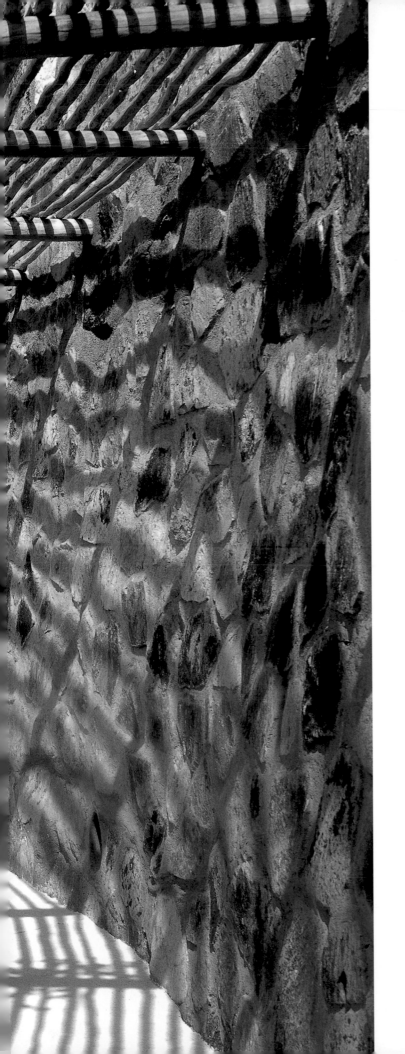

LA QUEBRADA

LA QUEBRADA, WHICH WAS DESIGNED BY Duccio Ermenegildo for himself, and is now owned by the British singer Seal, sits serenely on a cliff top in Costa Careyes with a 180-degree view of the Pacific. Ermenegildo is fond of visual surprises, and this house unveils itself stage by stage. "I wanted there to be a sense of discovery," he says. From the private lane that leads up to the property, the house is screened by high walls, as is the curved entry path that leads to a small piazza with a fountain. From the piazza, the thatched roof of the thirty-six-foot-high living and dining *palapa* and the bedroom tower reveal themselves. Between them a narrow stepped path edged with palms descends to the front terrace. Here the senses are fully awakened, for beyond the living areas is a cascade of steps opening onto a vast panorama of blue—the ocean, the pool, and the sky.

Ermenegildo has taken his inspiration from the work of Villaseñor and Aldaco but with a more rigorous modernist treatment. "My dream was to

LEFT This lower-level walk, which leads to a guest suite, was inspired by Ermenegildo's childhood memories of summers on the Amalfi coast in Italy.

217

marry minimalism with exotic local materials." The result, painted the orange of the poinciana flower, its edges defined by sinuous curves, is sensual and festive. Concrete is used for construction, and its organic properties are utilized for built-in banquettes in the living areas and in the bedrooms. Bathrooms have tubs molded from a mixture of powdered marble, granite chips, and cement, which was sanded and then waxed. Each bathroom has its own highly sculptural identity. The kitchen, as befits a designer who is also a chef, is built to gourmet standards and was a space much frequented by guests during Duccio's ownership.

A lower terrace below the pool, built into the cliff, leads to the guest bedrooms, and is a stylistic reminder of Duccio's childhood trips to the Amalfi coast in Italy.

LEFT The guest bedrooms, with master suite above (top). The living area (middle) has built-in seating and a side table. The dining area is above to the left; the palm-lined passage leads to the entry court. The *palapa* and the pool terrace (bottom). OPPOSITE The entry passage, flanked by high walls, leads into a small plaza with a cement-sided fountain filled with rocks. OVERLEAF The master bathroom is distinguished by strong, sculptural forms. A curved free-standing wall, mounted with twin showers on the front and washstands behind, divides the bathing and dressing areas. All surfaces are finished in sensuously smooth concrete—a mix of powdered marble, granite chips, and cement that is sanded and then waxed.

ABOVE LEFT A guest suite with high-level window vents. The built-in bench overlooks a balcony and the view. LEFT A guest bathroom has its own sculptural treatment. Again, the walls and circular tub are finished in a smooth, waxed cement. OPPOSITE The spectacular jacuzzi deck, hidden below the main pool-terrace level, is seen here at sunset. OVERLEAF The infinity-edged pool mimics the contours of the cliff with a sinuous S-curve.

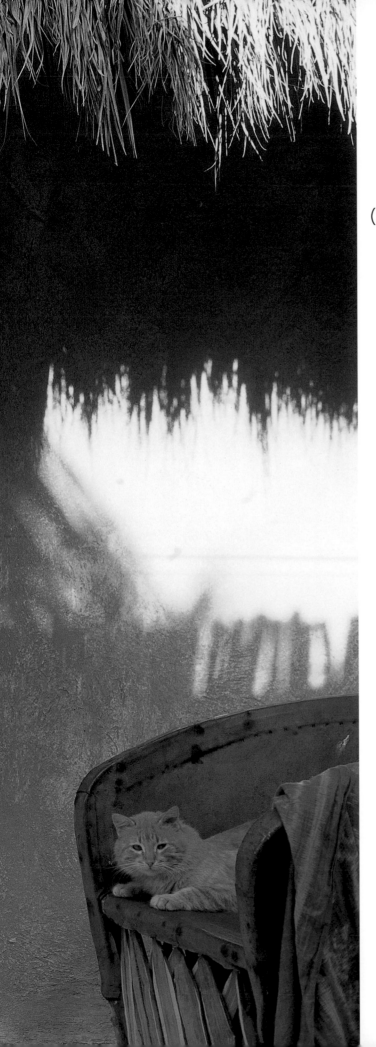

CASA COLIBRI
(THE HUMMINGBIRD HOUSE)
DESIGNER DUCCIO ERMENEGILDO

A VISIT TO CASA COLIBRI BEGINS WITH THE unusual. Passage into the garden from the entry gate is via a serpentine path tunneling through a giant copse of hibiscus, dramatically emerging in midlawn by the edge of a crisply designed pool and in front of the house itself.

Casa Colibri was the first venture in house design of Duccio Ermenegildo, an Italian who lives in New York and has a successful restaurant in Mexico City. He built it for himself, to provide a home base in Careyes. A house of interlocking courtyards and patios, it is set in a quiet lane not far from the Playa Rosa: The ocean can be glimpsed from the roof terrace.

From the front space, with its pool and grass, broad steps lead to a thatched living pavilion and a courtyard around which Casa Colibri's convivial life revolves. Radiating from the courtyard are the living, dining, sleeping, and kitchen areas, and from

LEFT The kitchen entrance leads to the dining space with its attendant cats. Rinky reclines patiently on an equipal, and Toukie stands near a stone utensil used for grinding corn.

227

her perch beside the dining table, Frida the parrot and self-appointed concierge keeps everyone entertained (but follows guests all the way to the gate when they leave). Behind the courtyard is another small patio, leading into the master suite; above which are guest bedrooms and a roof terrace.

Ermenegildo designed this house in a simpler, less folksy version of the Careyes style, distilled from his close connections with the New York art world and his attraction to minimalist design. Bathrooms are streamlined and bare, eschewing traditional Mexican tile for smooth-finished cement surfaces.

LEFT Oval cement stepping-stones (top) undulate across the back lawn to the staff cottage. This shaded dining space (middle) features a Mexican travertine table and Indonesian teak armchairs. Frida the parrot patrols a planter ledge (bottom). OPPOSITE The patio behind the dining area leads to bedrooms, a library, and a study. OVERLEAF The living room sofas and end tables are built into the concrete walls (left). Ermenegildo designed the bronze lamps and had them cast in Mexico City. Belén Esparsa, the cook, prepares lunch in the kitchen (right).

ABOVE LEFT The sitting area looks out onto the pool terrace. LEFT The kitchen terrace has a built-in pizza oven and equipal furniture. OPPOSITE The front terrace and pool. The living room is to the right, the kitchen to the left, and the bedrooms beyond. The folding *catre* benches are traditional Mexican folding cots. OVERLEAF The master bed (left) is covered with a gold-embroidered spread from India. Ermenegildo designed the wood bedside tables. The master bath (right) is open to the garden but partially screened by a cement wall.

TIGRE DEL MAR

ARCHITECT JEAN-CLAUDE GALIBERT

OVER THE YEARS, GIANFRANCO BRIGNONE, the padrone of Careyes, watched from Mi Ojo, his citadel overlooking the harbor, as the community he created grew from one house to a thriving town. A few years ago he decided to move on. He now lives in splendid isolation a few miles down the coast.

Gianfranco's new house, Tigre del Mar, is reached by an unpaved road that plunges through jungle, then passes a lagoon filled with water lilies and crocodiles, and emerges onto the rocky, cactus-covered headland.

Tigre del Mar was designed by Jean-Claude Galibert, but the bold flourishes are unmistakably those of Gianfranco himself. The blue tower first commands attention. Its verticality enables its owner to enjoy bird's-eye views of unspoiled beaches and of the network of lagoons behind. The house otherwise conforms to the usual Careyes pattern, with a large open-to-the-elements living *palapa* on one side, and an enclosed building—the blue tower—that contains the bedrooms, on the other. Between the two is a small plaza paved with a maze motif, and a large pool. Beyond these and the rocky, cactus-encrusted cliff, there is nothing to be seen of civilization except an occasional oil tanker passing along the horizon.

LEFT A view of the imposing silhouette of Tigre del Mar. The tower gives a spectacular view along the coast where turtles come by the hundreds to lay their eggs.

ABOVE Shaded built-in seating on the roof terrace is for relaxing and enjoying the view. RIGHT The breakfast terrace, also with built-in seating that is shaded from the sun, enjoys views of the lagoons behind the property. OVERLEAF A giant palapa, separate from the monolithic main building that houses the bedrooms, enfolds the living space, with a formal dining room above. There are spectacular views of the Pacific from its vantage point on this isolated headland.

BLANCANEAUX LODGE

ARCHITECT MANOLO MESTRE

MOST PEOPLE WHO TRAVEL TO BELIZE, A small, ecologically conscious country squeezed in between Guatemala and Mexico's Yucatán Peninsula, do so for the scuba diving; the world's second-largest barrier reef borders its coastline. They are often quite unaware of the attractive, undeveloped natural interior with its charming little towns and villages, tropical rain forests, and English-speaking population—a legacy from decades of British colonization.

Film director Francis Ford Coppola ventured to Belize in the early '80s, intrigued by this charming, peaceful, underpopulated country, and while visiting Pine Ridge Mountain Reserve was shown an abandoned lodge, which he bought and then forgot about for a few years. When he did return in a lull between projects, his interest reawakened, and he resolved to open up Blancaneaux, as it was now called, as a forty-five-acre hideaway resort and also to use for family holidays. He did this in two stages. First, in 1993, he renovated the lodge into its basic shape and opened it. Next, he extended it and

LEFT Guest villas, designed by Manolo Mestre and set in a forest of pine trees, overlook the Privasson River. The river descends through the Blancaneaux property in a succession of pools, rapids, and cascades.

added some tentative stylistic flourishes. It was then, in 1994, that he called in Manolo Mestre.

Mestre added additional thatched villas, nestling them in the pine-covered slopes overlooking the Privasson River, which cascades through the property in a series of waterfalls and lagoons. These structures, in typical Belizean fashion, are on stilts to catch the breeze and lessen the effects of humidity. They are framed entirely in recycled mahogany—which led Mestre to jokingly call them "the most luxurious structures in the world." The spaces between the framing are lined with palmetto (the stems of local palm) and plaster filling. An outside finish of palmetto helps the villas to merge with their surroundings. "The biggest compliment that Coppola received," Mestre recalls, "was from Dean Tavolaris, who said, 'It looks as if it was done by a local guy!'"

Floors were fabricated from local woods, which Mestre arranged in patterns to add interest. The colorful furnishings were found on buying trips that Mestre and Coppola made to Guatemala and Oaxaca. By the time they reached Oaxaca, the project had consumed Coppola so much that when Mestre, an expert on Mexican architecture, suggested they stop in to see the Iglesia de la Soledad, one of the most beautiful churches in Mexico, Coppola replied, "If I can't eat it or buy it, I don't want to see it!"

Blancaneaux is close to the ruins of Caracol, one of the largest Mayan cities, and only a few miles from Tikal, across the Guatemalan border. However, many visitors are content to enjoy the peace of the pine forests and swim in river water that is clean enough to drink.

OPPOSITE A suite decorated with colorful fabrics from neighboring Guatemala, Mexican furniture, masks, and animal figures. The upper walls are lined with bamboo. RIGHT The design of this guest cottage (top) echoes the traditional design; the hammock is Mexican. The bedroom (middle) overlooks a waterfall. A shower stall (bottom) is lined with Mexican tile and extends beyond the roof thatch for open-air bathing.

ABOVE LEFT A guest cottage, again furnished with Guatemalan fabrics. LEFT This guest bedroom has wood-shuttered
windows; the floor is made from two hardwoods, alternated
to give a striped effect. OPPOSITE In the renovated original
lodge, a Mexican wood figure decorates the stone bar counter,
which is incised with pre-Colombian motifs.

ACKNOWLEDGMENTS

I AM FORTUNATE IN THAT many of the people whose houses are featured in this book are friends, so this book represents a visual diary of my life and travels over the last ten years. I am grateful to all of them for their wonderful hospitality and opportunities to enjoy their wonderful houses.

I am particularly grateful to the staff of *Architectural Digest* magazine, who very kindly allowed me to use a number of photos that were originally included in features on Jaya Ibrahim's two houses, the Begawan Giri resort, Linda Garland's Panchoran, the Villa Bebek, Amir Rabik's compound, John Hardy's residence, La Quebrada, and Blancaneaux Lodge.

My special thanks to my muse and mentor in all things cultural, Made Wijaya, and the architect Manolo Mestre, whose hospitality and support over the years was invaluable. Special thanks also to longtime friends Jan Sharp and Philip Noyce for help in Jamaica and their hospitality during editing.

Thanks also to Duccio Ermenegildo, Seal, Mari-Carmen Hernandez, Isabel Goldsmith, Giorgio and Ana Brignone, and Gianfranco Brignone in Mexico; Tony and Wendy Hart, Blaise Hart, Perry and Sally Henzell, Romana Fabbris, Chris Salewicz, Chris Blackwell, and Deborah Yaeger of Island Outposts in Jamaica; Mary Anne McIntyre, Joel Pauleau, Warwick Purser, Mubarak, Hans Hoefer, Charley Hulse, and Channa Daswatte in Sri Lanka; Jaya Ibrahim and his mother, John Saunders, and Soedarmadji Damais in Java; Made Wijaya, Sri Sudewi, Linda Garland, John and Cynthia Hardy, Putu Suarsa, Cheong Yew Kuan, Bradley Gardner, Hugo Jereissati, and Idanna Pucci in Bali; and in Belize, Francis Ford Coppola.

In the States, thanks to Mike Kelly for his tech support, Richard Ferretti for the stylish design job on this book, and especially to my illustrious editor, Roy Finamore—this is our fourth book together!

And finally to my wife, Annie Kelly, who was heartbroken that she had to stay home.

RESOURCES

The following is a list of resorts and houses featured in these pages available for rent.

JAMAICA

Good Hope Villa. Call (876) 610-5798.

Strawberry Hill. Call Island Outposts reservations, (800) 688-7678,
  or the resort direct, (876) 944-8400, fax (876) 944-8408.

Goldeneye. Call Island Outposts reservations, (800) 688-7678,
  or the resort direct, (876) 975-3354, fax (876) 975-3620.

Round Hill Hotel and Villas. Call (876) 956-7050, fax (876) 956-7505.

SRI LANKA

Hans Hoefer's beach villa and Illukitaya, his plantation house.
  Contact by internet at www.hoefernet.com

The Sunhouse, Taprobane, or Tangalle. Call or fax 949-22624, or 9474-380275.

BALI

Taman Bebek Villas. Call 62361-975-385, fax 62361-976-532.

The House at Iseh. Contact c/o Bali Tropical Villas, 62361-732083.

Begawan Giri Resort. Call 62361-978-888 or e-mail Western Oriental at
  info@westernoriental.com.

Panchoran estate. Call Western Oriental, London (44171) 207-313-6600,
  fax (44171) 207-313-6601.

MEXICO

Costa Careyes Hotel and Casitas de las Flores (villas also available).
  Call (52) 335-10240, fax 335-10246.

Las Alamandas. Call (888) 882-9616.

BELIZE

Blancaneaux Lodge. Call (501) 92-3878, fax (501) 92-3919.

INDEX

Page numbers in *italics* refer to captions.